Trespasses

sightline books

The Iowa Series in Literary Nonfiction

Patricia Hampl & Carl H. Klaus, series editors

Lacy M. Johnson
Trespasses

A Memoir

University of Iowa Press, Iowa City

University of Iowa Press, Iowa City 52242
www.uiowapress.org
Printed in the United States of America
Text design by Richard Hendel

The University of Iowa Press is a member of Green
Press Initiative and is committed to preserving
natural resources.
Printed on acid-free paper

Library of Congress
Cataloging-in-Publication Data
Johnson, Lacy M., 1978–
Trespasses: a memoir / Lacy M. Johnson
    p.   cm.—(Sightline books. The Iowa series in
literary nonfiction)
Includes bibliographical references.
ISBN-13: 978-1-60938-078-6, ISBN-10: 1-60938-078-9 (pbk)
ISBN-13: 978-1-60938-095-3, ISBN-10: 1-60938-095-9 (ebook)
1. Johnson, Lacy M., 1978–   2. Macon (Mo.)—Biography.
I. Title.
F474.M315J64 2012
977.8'27—dc23
                                    2011037694

FOR HAZEL

Our Father, who art in heaven,

hallowed be thy name.

Thy kingdom come.

Thy will be done,

on earth as it is in heaven.

Give us this day our daily bread,

and forgive us our trespasses,

as we forgive those who trespass against us,

and lead us not into temptation,

but deliver us from evil.

For thine is the kingdom,

the power, and the glory for ever.

Amen.

contents

In the summer of 2006, my husband and I packed up our Jeep and drove from our apartment in Houston, Texas, to my childhood home in Macon, Missouri—nearly a thousand miles—and filmed over sixty hours of interviews with my parents, grandparents, aunts, uncles, and siblings, many of whom still reside in the sparsely populated county where my family has lived for the past 180 years. Much of the material in this book has been pulled from those interviews. At first, I dedicated a lot of time to transcribing the interviews. I focused on getting the details right, sticking to the facts. Then I stopped. Because I know these stories like I know my reflection in a mirror. And at a certain point the facts got in the way of the truth.*

Asterisks indicate notes at the back of the book.

Trespasses

rural route one

You live with your mama and daddy, two sisters, three dogs, two horses, and exactly twelve cats on a farm* so far from town you barely see the street lights' bright white tossed over the horizon. Your mama grows a garden of fresh green vegetables right outside your back door and you and your sisters pick peas and tomatoes in the afternoon while Mama hangs clean white sheets on the clothesline and the hot sun freckles your shoulders with small brown spots. The vegetables snap so easy from the vines and their sun-warm juices run down your chin and into your hands while the sweet groundwater sticks to your tongue. You wash up at the water pump while the bird dogs yap from their pens and when nobody's looking you lie down in the long uncut grass behind the barn, where you can close your eyes and spread your whole body out under the sky's blue curve. When your daddy comes up to the house all sweating and covered in hay-seed you set the table and make sure the silverware's in all the right places or you have to drink water with your dinner instead of tea.

1

2006

Days before my husband and I load our suitcases into the car and drive from our apartment in Houston, Texas, to my childhood home in Macon, Missouri, I have an argument with a New Yorker. *The problem with midwesterners,* he tells me, *is that you have no culture.** He has come to this conclusion after having driven through the Midwest at some point in the past. His scalp shines through his hair in the patio light, which glints off the glasses he wears pushed far up on his nose. *Applebee's,* he says, crossing his legs at the knees, *is not culture.* I do not spit in his face.

Because he's right, of course: Applebee's is not culture. But what makes me angry is that he associates Applebee's with me. My hometown doesn't have an Applebee's, but the restaurants you'll see from the highway include McDonald's, Hardee's, Taco Bell, Burger King, Sonic, and KFC. From the highway, you are also likely to see our big-box stores, which include several regional chain grocery stores and a Wal-Mart, which opened the same year my family moved to town, and which, when I was in high school, gave me a job when there were no other jobs to be had, a job which allowed me to put myself through college, pay my rent, keep my car running, and put groceries in my fridge. Over the years, many small businesses in town shuttered their doors, perhaps as a result of Wal-Mart, or perhaps as a result of the failing economy. One of the few businesses that continued to thrive, despite the presence of Wal-Mart, was Ben Franklin, a five-and-dime downtown. After school, mom would drag my sisters and me to Ben Franklin while she shopped for fabric. We'd follow her around, tugging at the neatly stacked bolts, until we got bored and she got irritated. I always found my way to the button aisle, where a whole wall of buttons stared back at me for hours.

So yes, I get angry with the New Yorker who says we have no

culture. Because he's only looking at the surface. While it's true that many people in my hometown may not object to their choices in retail or restaurants — after all, it's our God-given right to shop at Wal-Mart, where we can buy guns and ammo and diapers and formula under one roof—that's not to say that doing so strips us of culture. Because if you leave the highway, you'll find locally owned restaurants, where the cooks prepare quail on Sundays and fried frog legs Friday night.*

It's all very American, I tell him. And by this I also mean the regional chain of grocery stores, the Wal-Mart, even Applebee's, even though that's all he sees. Like algae on the surface of a pond. To get the clean, fresh water underneath you have to break through that surface. *My culture is like that*, I tell him. And for the first time, I believe it.

1944

Arthur couldn't know about the grape arbor unless he also knows about Wilda Eloise taunting the bull from the mulberry tree, finally growing too scared to run for the fence because after all it wouldn't hold when that bull had gotten so mad as to be stamping and snorting and running his horns up and down the trunk, the bark flying off like hornets in every direction. And Arthur wouldn't know about that mulberry tree unless he also knows about the photograph of her mother, a twin, as an infant, and how the younger twin died so young of a burst appendix, *a shame to lose the better one*, everyone said. And if he knows about that photograph then he also knows about the Jimtown* school, has sat in its one bright-lit room, a light layer of chalk dust on every surface but the wood-burning stove—soot-pail black, stovepipe black, burner-door black—so black its shadow darkens even the southwesternmost desk, where she traced her initials into the woodgrain every afternoon of every year. And if he knows about that desk, then he also knows about the bend in the road between their houses, how the trees lean over like a bridge where the underbrush grows so thick and so tall you can hear but not see that a creek also bends there, the water babbling so long it's made the stones smooth as a whisper on both sides. He asks for her hand because he knows that place, and that the only thing she could love more than her mama and daddy and brother is a man who will never tell her anything except that she is beautiful, so they drive all night across the border where the judges don't know she's only sixteen,* and the whole way back she leans into his shoulder, rubbing her fingers over his knuckles on the wheel.

still life with coffee

woman walks into the beauty salon at the same time on the same day every week, and every week she says *good morning* to the same set of women in the same set of chairs, and every time the same set of women stand over them with the same set of hair picks and perm rods and sharp-gleaming scissors. The woman says *good morning* and lumbers toward her empty chair, second from the end, which is turned toward her, to face her, to welcome her enormous weight to its margarine vinyl seat. She says *good morning* and sits down, holding her enormous beige purse on her lap, allowing the woman standing behind to wrap a pink vinyl cape around her shoulders, not snapping it closed, but letting it drape there for a moment while she fetches a black plastic jaw clip from her drawer. The woman's shoulders settling into position, her hands resting over the brass clasp of her purse, her feet pulling up to the foot rest, she gradually tunes in to the day's conversation, which is the same conversation at this same time on this same day every week: *You know their mother feeds them cereal for break-fast . . . no kind of God-fearing woman I know . . . and to think: her own kin . . . in her housecoat . . . and she told my friend who told me . . . with a man from her Bible study.* Meanwhile, a fly buzzes in and out of the chemical fumes wafting from open bottles on the countertop, lands on the stained lip of a coffee cup, alights again when the woman reaches for her drink. Outside, her husband waits in the car with the windows down, the motor's heat still shimmering off the hood, half-listening to the farm report, hoping the feeder cattle futures are off. He applies a thin coat of Chapstick while he squints into the sun. *These things happen*, the woman says, waving the fly off her coffee cup. *But goodness knows* — she takes a sip — *I'm not one to talk.*

5

1945

When the mail carrier pulls his dusty white truck over to the side of the road and slips a stack of envelopes in the rusty hollow of the mailbox's iron mouth, Wilda Eloise has already run halfway down the driveway, a white cotton dishrag in each hand. The whole family's been hanging around the porch all day, occasionally wandering off to half-complete some otherwise necessary chore — leaving cows half-milked, corn half-shucked, fence half-mended — returning to watch the REA* linemen finally string the long black wire from the government pole to the family's four-room house. Her father wired every room weeks ago — soon as the men had come out to set the pole — stringing a single light from the center of every ceiling, rushing down to the co-op days later to buy an electric icebox and a fan. But the linemen's work is slow and she walks around the corner of the house to lean against its shadow — the wood planks smooth and cool against her shoulder — and opens the letter from her husband, now a cryptographer in the army, stationed in Africa since March. Inside, a love poem he's clipped from the newspaper.*

Her father's gone from the porch when she rounds the corner, climbs the stairs, and pulls open the front door of the house, the clipping cradled in her palm. Inside, both her parents sit at the kitchen table, staring blankly at the new appliances, every blind in the house drawn closed. In the parlor, the radio plays the news — *the battleship Missouri, 53,000-ton flagship of Admiral Halsey's Third Fleet, becomes the scene of an unforgettable ceremony marking the complete and formal surrender of Japan* — while water boils on the stove. She returns the clipping to the envelope, folds it discreetly, tucks it into the pocket of her apron, and turns toward her room to hide it away. And then the fan sputters and begins turning. The refrigerator clicks, hums, and begins whirring. For a moment the family is silent. Then her mother cries out — for joy!—a smile cracks the leather of her father's face, their chairs toppling as they shoot to their feet, the glasses rattling in the cupboard, the cans clanking together on the shelves, the whole kitchen dancing in the dim glow of the light bulb overhead. Even the shadows on the floor throw back their heads and shout with glee.

2006

When we arrive in town, we stop at the house on Jackson Street to unpack. On the outside it looks roughly the same. My mom got the house in the divorce, and each Christmas my sisters and I used to return here, sleeping all together in my old bedroom upstairs, sneaking cigarettes out the window for nostalgia's sake, reminiscing until our words ran together, and our giggles became slow breathing became sleep. But even then it wasn't the house in which I'd spent my teenage years—several rooms closed off with heavy blankets, a couch pulled into the dining room, half of the furniture gone. When my mom remarried and decided to sell the house, my dad's new wife saw the potential for a little real estate gain and talked my dad into buying the house a second time. They closed a few weeks ago, but won't move in until next month. They've brought over a bed, a TV, a DVD player, and a couple of chairs for us to use while we're in town, bringing the house's emptiness into sharp relief: my mom's floral-print wallpaper half pulled down, half the rooms half repainted, flowers still blooming in the garden, the grass going to seed, no one around to mow.

There's very little to do tonight in the in-between house. We could look at photos my husband took on the drive from Texas. We could grab dinner at any of the fast-food restaurants lining Macon's one major street, bring it home, and eat it on the porch swing. Under any other circumstances, I might call this evening boring, but small town life operates at a slower pace than we're used to and there's no choice but to fall into step. It doesn't take me long to remember the rhythm. Growing up on a farm north of town, I spent very little time feeling bored. Instead, I'd wander out to the horse pasture, or down to the creek bottom, tell my mom or my dad I was going, and just leave. Whole afternoons spent poking through a pile of sticks. No one worried about me because I knew the rules: don't do anything stupid and if you do, finish it before dark. *I would never let my grandsons do that*, my dad tells me during his interview. *Because now we just have so much more knowledge about the bad activities of society. Things move faster than they used to.*

But on the porch swing, life moves slowly. Thunder announces the approaching storm and my husband saunters into the house to get his camera, bending to collect our trash from dinner on the way. He takes his time setting the camera up on the tripod, makes another trip into the house to get a couple of chairs. It's an hour before the lightning comes. Another hour before the rain. We don't capture more than a handful of pictures of the dark sky splitting open over our heads, though we spend the whole evening trying.

1947

For near as long as she can remember, Laura Anna's job on the family farm has been milking the cows. Her twelve siblings (three brothers, nine sisters) divide the other chores: the boys tend the cattle and the row crops, while the girls feed the chickens and keep the house. When Laura Anna returns to the farm from school each day, she hangs her school clothes neatly on wooden hangers and smoothes the wrinkles out of the pressed cotton fabric, before tying her hair up under a rag and pulling on her mucking clothes. The fourth-youngest child of a hot-headed woman and a hard-handed man, she's learned to keep her comings and goings quiet. Invisible. A ghost. She tiptoes down the stairs, past the kitchen's chorus of shuffling skirts, to the back door, where she sidles her white-socked feet into a pair of barn boots, too big for her—a brother's maybe—but the only ones that are free. The screen door creaks as she opens it. The shuffles silence. A voice calls from the kitchen— *You there. Girl. Run down to the cellar and get me . . .* —but she's out the door and running across the crisp brown lawn before her mother can finish the sentence.

Out in the barn, Laura Anna finds, if nothing else, a little privacy. Beyond the occasional brother coming in to pull down an extra bridle or a yoke, Laura has the place to herself. She hates the chore of milking—twice a day, every day—but there's something comforting and familiar in the ritual: the low three-legged stool, the dull fat-filmy bucket, the warm udder softening under her touch. The bucket fills in long, rhythmic streams, air bubbles collecting and dispersing on the milk's smooth surface. This milk is meant for tonight's dinner: folded into flour for biscuits, whisked with bacon fat into gravy, poured into several short glasses for the youngest sisters.

This weekend they'll churn butter in the barn, curdle the milk into cheese, fill giant barrels with thick, warm milk, and watch their brothers drive it into town. On their way back into the house, the sisters will walk past their father on the porch: he will tip his chair backward against the house's outer wall, wiping the sweat from his upper lip with a handkerchief, tucking it back into his hip pocket. None of them will look him in the eye.

But today, a beige two-door Studebaker pulls into the drive. The milk tester. Laura Anna leans deeper into her stool, keeps her head down as the dark-haired man comes into the barn, opens his redrusted toolbox, pulls out a couple of dingy glass vials, wipes them on his shirt. *Afternoon*, he says, dipping a vial into her bucket. *Mmph*, she responds, leaning out of his way, wiping her hands on the legs of her pants. He agitates the vial between his fingers, turns toward the light and holds it close to his eye. After a few moments a layer of fat balloons to the surface. *Afternoon*, he says, packs up his vials, and drives away.

Harold, twenty, just home from the war, tests the milk from dairies all over Clark County. Photographs from that time show a man with black wavy hair, combed back and waxed just so, or with a lock pulled messily downward from the center, the sun-weathered skin on his forehead charging forward: a scorpion, a bull. His dark eyes cast in shadow. As he tells it, *I would never say she was pretty, but she had this crooked smile that made her look kind of interesting. And she was the only skinny one there. And, well, I liked 'em skinny.* He's gruff and loud and bossy, and even then his meanness, deep and good-humored as it may be, appeals to Laura Anna on some level. Shy and reclusive, beaten by one parent or sibling or another, she's got nothing to lose. One Sunday evening he shows up in his Studebaker and she comes down to the front door with her suitcase packed. She turns to the dining room, where the whole family eats in silence. No one looks up as she walks out the door.*

1990

My sisters and I spill from our van into the front yard, choosing separate paths through the labyrinth of musty furniture, pausing at the occasional card tables to finger some yellowed knickknack, finding our mutual way toward the porch. Inside the dark house,* where no one has thought to open a window, even the air smells unused, like sweaters forgotten too many seasons in a cardboard box, like a closet under the stairs. My aunts and uncles carry boxes from room to room. My sisters and I scurry away from the commotion, up the stairs to the second floor, where our great aunt cries into a bedspread, up the stairs to the attic, where we find our cousins elbow-deep in a dusty steamer trunk: a fur stole, a partially crushed hat, its fishnet veil stiff and gummy, a stack of tiny lace gloves. Outside, the auctioneer starts calling for bids. In a corner, we find a box of postcards and letters, conversations between people I will never know about the weather, their children, the events of an uneventful day.

At the funeral the next morning, we sit quietly. We do not speak, or if we speak it is only in a whisper. Because we are family, we sit in a private room. My cousin and I peek through the partition to see the congregation in the main hall. Old women. Old men. How will they remember this woman who has died? Months ago my sisters and I visited her in the nursing home. She kept calling us the wrong names, thought it was a different year, accused my little sister of being a boy. *We're Barry's daughters,* my sister told her. *Arthur and Wilda's grandchildren.* Eventually she gave up trying to place us, asked if we had any candy.

Now, it's our turn to pay our respects. My cousins and I stand, walk slowly toward the casket. Her body looks nothing like a living person. I'm tempted to touch her hand, but I know how it will feel: cold as the nursing-home floor. Back in our seats, my cousins begin squirming. We're ready to go back to my grandmother's house for the wake: to change out of our church clothes and run in the yard without shoes. The women from the church will bring food. Our parents will sit around the dining table drinking coffee, the women laughing a little too loudly. I will stand over a table crowded with casseroles, an empty plate in my hand. With my eyes closed I can already feel the sun on my face, my skin starting to tighten under the burn.

1950

Laura Anna makes a few absentminded trips up the narrow stairwell from the kitchen to open a window at the end of the hallway, to close a creaking door. Two parallel tire paths connect the four-square farmhouse in Missouri to the end of the winding drive — their mailbox, its black shuttered mouth, its saluting red hand, across the border in Iowa. She feels that way, too, sometimes. As if she's always straddling something — one part of her in this place, another part across some invisible border. The doctors have forbidden her to get out of bed, but she doesn't listen, instead continues cooking every meal, tidying the house, keeping up with her outdoor chores.

As a child she taught herself to sew and knit and crochet, and by now she's fitted every window with sunny yellow curtains, her husband with a handsome linen suitcoat lined in striped gray satin, the baby's room with small, bright blankets and clothes. It's not much, but it makes life a little more comfortable, and she could never afford to buy these things from a store. Years later she'll teach her daughter, my mother, these same skills, sitting beside her at the machine, pressing lightly on the foot pedal, guiding the fabric with a gentle hand. *It's a skill you ought to know.*

That afternoon, in the farmhouse on the border between Missouri and Iowa, Laura Anna can't help pacing, a restless instinct that tells her it's nearly time. When the first pain hits, she boils water and pulls a stack of towels down from the cedar closet. When her water breaks, she almost goes outside to dig a hole. In one version of the story, Harold comes with the Studebaker to take her to the doctor just in time, just as she's climbing down into the washtub to start pushing. In another version, she's never been more alone.

In October, a month later, Laura Anna's already out in the barn milking the cow, feeding the chickens, slopping the pigs, while the baby—a red-headed girl she's named Judith Marlene*—sleeps in the house or in a basket on the porch. They don't have any money saved—no one around here makes any—and they don't need it just now. When Judy gets a little older, starts getting into things, Laura Anna arranges with a neighbor to watch her daughter a couple of hours a week in exchange for doing her laundry. *Don't worry*, the neighbor assures her, *I'll watch her like one of my own.* The days she leaves Judy next door, Laura grows quieter than usual, takes longer to do her chores, sometimes stopping to stare out past where the blackberries grow wild along the unfenced edge of the property line, across some unreachable distance.

inside joke

A man walks up to a bar. Says, *all the heroes are gone.* Says, *some left town with the others and some just keep to themselves.* The rest are forgotten, either purposefully — locked away and ignored forever — or by some accident of popularity or time. If they resurface, unexpected and unwelcome, they knock at the door just as the wife's put dinner on the table, and won't take *nothankyou* for an answer, rapping at the open windows, barking to be let in. Bottled up, bottled in, the shadow of a former self making change behind the counter, wandering away from the tiller in the middle of the afternoon, a pair of calloused hands pouring from the frayed spouts of shirt cuffs, dirty fingernails scratching at mud-flecked skin. Davy Crockett. Marshal Dillon. The names repeated by a radio mounted on the wall behind the bar. The Lone Ranger. He spits tobacco from the corner of his mouth. His faithful sidekick. Who is that masked man? Their deaths have left his soul a little warped. Then the wife comes into the room and wants to know where the money is. The daughter needs a new dress. The son needs a pair of shoes. It'll never be the same again, you know. One day the hero rode off into the sunset and shot his horse beneath a blooming tree. Now the daughter wants to hold hands crossing the street. The son walks an imaginary dog on a leash. The bartender rolls his eyes. *I'll remember this years from now,* he says, *the moment you saddle up your horse.* The man says, *No,* drinks his whiskey, *I want to forget.* The flowering tree. Her hand. The leash.

1986

It's mid-July when Judy packs her three children and their small suitcases into the beige conversion van and drives three hours from her home in Muscatine, Iowa, to her parents' home in Unionville, Missouri. I'm seven, my older sister, Lisa, is twelve, and our younger sister, Leeanne, is four. The plan, Grandma Laura tells us as she turns up the knob on the air-conditioning unit mounted in the wall, is we'll stay for a week. Leeanne starts to cry. Lisa rolls her eyes.

Our grandparents don't keep toys in their house for us to play with — this is the first time we've visited by ourselves for any length of time — so we've brought a few of the Barbies and Cabbage Patch dolls we share at home to keep Leeanne entertained, though in the crowded rooms of the small tidy house, she doesn't have space to play with them. And because Harold and Laura live in rural Missouri, they don't have cable either. Instead, they have an aerial antenna mounted on the roof.* It's motorized and connected to a fist-sized dial on top of the console in the den: east for ABC, south for NBC, west for CBS. In the morning, Grandma keeps us busy watching the *Today Show* while she rinses our breakfast dishes and washes our laundry, and in the afternoons she lets us help weed her shady garden behind the house. After dinner, we sit under the fan at the kitchen table playing Old Maid while Grandpa snores in his recliner, the police scanner blaring beside him. He eats dinner with us, and lunch, but the rest of the time he's out in the work building, where we are not allowed to go.

As the middle child, it's my job to keep the peace, and I refrain from playing with Leeanne and her dolls, or from watching television with Lisa, so I can monitor everything that's going on. Distanced — that's what I'd call it now. Vigilant. Nervous. My parents have been acting strange, and I must sense there's something going on, because I'm always sitting near Grandma in the kitchen, at the bar, where I can see the whole length of the house. If I could I'd climb the brick-paneled walls and perch at the top of the hutch. I don't sleep well in this house, in my mother's old room, her adolescent ghost too much for me to take in. Grandma thinks I'm hungry, or thirsty, all this lingering, and keeps offering me something to eat or drink. But I'm not hungry or thirsty, I'm poised to intercept complaints. At the first sign of a bored or cranky sibling, I'll swoop in and save the day. After three whole days of this, Grandma's had enough. After lunch, she shoos the three of us into the truck, hands Grandpa the keys, tells us to *Get lost.*

And that's exactly what he does. He drives in loopy circles in the general direction of downtown. We don't pay attention to where he's turned, the names of any of the streets. We look out the windows, enjoy the breeze through the open windows, scan for signs of other children: a park, a jungle gym, a ball rolling into the street. After twenty minutes of circling, Grandpa pulls into the Dairy Lane, where he buys us each an ice cream cone dipped in chocolate, which hardens quickly into a brittle candy shell. A miracle, it seems, until the ice cream is melting and running into our hands, dripping from our elbows to the smooth cement floor. Grandpa finishes first, wipes his mouth, and then climbs in the truck, waves to us, and leaves.

For the first few minutes we're stunned. We stay in our spots on the peeling picnic benches, moving only to fetch Leeanne a wad of wet napkins. Lisa bets he'll get back to the house and once he tells Grandma what he's done, she'll send him straight back to get us. *For sure.* Fifteen minutes pass. Thirty. At last she grabs each of our sticky hands—mine and Leeanne's—and starts off in what we believe to be the direction of the house.

After two hours walking in the blistering heat, we spot a diner, where we ask the cashier for a glass of water. She is a stout woman with orange hair, a black mole painted on her cheek, a cigarette dangling from the hand she raises from her hip to her coffee-yellowed teeth. Her eyebrows, penciled on in a too-dark shade, wrinkle upward unnaturally. She asks who we are and where on earth we think we are going. *Laura and Harold Webber? Why, they're just up the hill.*

As Grandpa tells it now, he had just climbed back into the truck to look for us when he spotted our three wilted bodies limping up the street. I remember it differently: Grandma meets us at the door with a cool towel, wipes us down—each forehead, each arm, the back of each neck—leads us out to the porch and pours us each a glass of lemonade. We are mad and tired and exhilarated, and more than a little bewildered by how hard and how long Grandpa laughs at the sight of us while leaning far back into his iron patio chair, sipping his sweet iced tea.

2006

Just as when I ask him about the plane, rubbing the stubble on his chin as he scans his memory, letting his eyes drift toward the ceiling, his hands a little away from his body, before catching himself and snapping back into his closely ordered place. The plane—which he still flies, and which he built from scratch over fifteen years: the engine out in the garage, the wings in the upstairs bedrooms after the children moved away (he had to take off part of the upstairs wall to lower them, finished, to the ground), the body out in the work building, once he'd built that, too—is now stored in the hangar at the airport, fifteen miles northwest of town. He flies it when he can, weekly sometimes, when he's feeling up to it. His hips cause him a lot of pain, the cartilage ground away over decades of hard labor, though he's reluctant to admit it. The pain doesn't stop him from getting up each morning and shuffling out to the shop, as he calls it—a giant barnlike edifice, its corrugated metal siding crisp and shining behind the house, casting reflections into my grandmother's garden, lighting her birdhouses from unnatural angles. These days his shop overflows with half-assembled tractors—spare engine parts piled haphazardly in barrels, leaking oil like some scene of postindustrial gore. Out of the spares, he builds motors of his own invention—greasy, metal Frankenstein monsters that spit fire and oil and a rough, percussive music. Leaning a little forward in his chair, to the side, on his good hip, he tells me, *Of course I still remember the first plane I saw:* a postal that flew daily over his father's farm. Each day he folded his body toward the ground to tend the field; each afternoon he straightened up to watch the plane cut through the sky.

still life with bacon

Next he drives her to the butcher shop,* where a forged iron bell above the door clangs when the woman enters, and where the black-and-white checkered tile floor does not gleam or squeak under the woman's orthopedic shoes, though the floor is mopped at the end of each and every day, and where the butcher himself stands behind the counter, or hunches, rather, chin-deep in the display case, rotating the meat toward a fresher presentation — rump roast to the front, stew meat to the rear, t-bones and butterfly chops stacked four high at center stage. He gives her a wide smile, a regular customer, wipes his hands on the front of his apron, says, *What can I get for you?* She clears her throat. *The usual*, she says. As it happens, he was just about to restock the bacon. Still a little low from Saturday, you see. Says, *Let me just.* And by this he means: pass through the double swinging doors into the cooler, and through the cooler to the deep freeze, where the breath snows back in the face, where the cattle ramp is visible out the sometimes-open door, where the lowing can be sometimes heard while the cattle unload, descending the rickety ramp on mud-caked hoofs, to be drained, flayed, strung up on hooks. He emerges into the shop front, the cold air trailing behind him, wraps her bacon in clean white paper. *What else can I get for you?* he asks, smiling the same polite smile. *You can tell me*, she says in her most fly-catching voice, *why your family hasn't been to church in a month of Sundays.* Well if that don't beat all. Oh, the kids, he might say. The hours. The wife. The car. It's calving season. A load of pork to carve. A jammed sausage stuffer. Took the whole weekend to fix. She smiles the polite smile. *Have a good day*, she says. And by this she means.

rural route one

You attend second service every Sunday and sometimes Wednesday nights since the day you are born and Brother Dan or Brother Darrell preaches about the glory and grace of Jesus Christ and you accept Him as your Lord and Savior or you burn in hell and this is why you've been baptized twice and saved exactly twenty-seven times.* Every week your mama and you and your sisters get real dressed up in the pretty cotton dresses she makes special for wearing to church. Your mama's always made all your clothes special with her own two hands and you are grateful for each hem until the rich kids in your Sunday school don't look at you even when you sit right next to them. Your daddy says vanity's an expensive sin but sometimes your mama drives you and your sisters to Wal-Mart anyway and she buys you underwear and socks and a pair of Lee jeans that are exactly two inches shorter than your legs and she presses her lips real tight together the whole time. One day she stops making pretty cotton dresses but the rich kids still don't look at you. They never look at you.

2006

ornings the bedroom fills with light, muted only a little by the drawn white curtains. Floorboards unbuckle and settle under the anchor of my weight padding stiffly toward the bathroom (the first diurnal gesture, washing and rewashing, squinting into the streaked and spotted mirror), before the water rushes downward and away toward some extinct system of pipes and creeks, streams, and rivers, to irrigate some black-bottomed field. The door sticks and creaks on its slightly slouching jamb, continues creaking as I poke my husband—*Scooch over*—and climb back into bed. The move we know so well: my back against his chest, his face between my shoulder blades, our bodies spooned together like two s's, his arm under my arm, over and around my belly, where our unborn child begins to stir inside me. He drifts back to sleep while I watch the day arrive through the curtains and consider the several possible trajectories of our life: Our life in a city, with museums and subways and ballet classes for our daughter. Our life on a farm, with forests and a barn and our own egg-laying hens.

I've asked each person during the interview what they would want our unborn child to know about them. Each time the same response: *That I love her.* This is not the answer I'm looking for. Maybe because the question is really: What do I want her to know about me? More important, what do I know about me? In many ways, this question is just another way of asking something we all eventually wonder: Who am I and where do I come from?

If you'd asked me this question when I last lived in this house I would have changed the subject. Because, you see, my family's been living here so long no one remembers anyone having been from anywhere else. For a history class I took in college I was supposed to write a paper about how my family came to America. Too ashamed to tell the truth—*I don't know*—I made up a story instead using bits and pieces from my favorite historical narratives: Irish farmers who emigrated during the potato blight, German stowaways who worked their way across the country on the railroad, forty acres and a mule. The fact is, no one thought our history was important enough to tell it and keep telling. For a long time, I agreed.

And then a chain-link gate creaks to in a yard down the street. My husband coughs, resettles. I consider getting out of bed. Our daughter turns a somersault inside me: the nucleus of history uncocooning, a small, live thing taking form.

1952

The kitchen hangs suspended in perpetual summer while Wilda wipes a hand on her apron, and pushes back her hair with the clean side of her wrist, a motion which does not go unnoticed by Arthur, who passes through with no clear purpose but to kiss her neck as she checks the green beans and bacon, a kiss she leans into with the lid in one hand, a wooden spoon in the other. He kisses her neck and then takes a bottle opener from the drawer by the sink and brings it to his father, Arthur Sr., on the south-facing porch, where all other sounds drown in the woodenness of the two chairs creaking: a sudden, oaky groan as Arthur Jr. first sits down, then two mapley grunts as the men lean together, each stretching an arm toward the other: Arthur Sr. offering the bottle in his hand, Arthur Jr. taking hold of it, popping off its cap, which plunks to the floorboards and rolls toward where his second son, Barry, pushes a shiny green tractor through the dust: a gift from the older man. And then there is only the occasional creak of a chair: the younger Arthur with his feet planted firmly on the floor, the fingers of one hand curled around the worn arm, his head leaned back into the afternoon light, making a shadow of his dark skin, the other hand raising the dewy bottle to his lips at regular intervals. The older Arthur, whose legs do not reach to the floor, but stop abruptly above the knees in clean-bandaged stumps,* keeps his head upright, his eyes open, his free hand in a near-fist on his lap. A laugh from the kitchen pulls the younger Arthur out of his trance, back to his feet, up out of his chair. He sets the bottle down on the plank table between them and reenters the house. His father keeps their time alone, lifts the bottle to his lips, takes a drink, lets his attention fall toward Barry on the floor, who does not play with the tractor in the dust but instead eyes the abandoned bottle on the table, his tongue passing over his lips, between his white corn-kernel teeth. The fist on the man's lap uncurls, turns over, blooms like a flower, a motion that says to the boy, *Come here*. The cool glass bottle against his mouth, a warm gentle hand on the back of his head: sassafras, Old Spice, sarsaparilla. He winks at his grandson before recasting his gaze beyond the row of houses across the street. The boy turns to look too, sees only dust swirling in the afternoon light.

1986

My sister hogs the covers most nights, sleeps in the middle of the full-size mattress, the sheets wrapped several times around her, the comforter cast off her side of the bed. In the morning, my father wakes before the alarm sounds, stumbles into the bathroom, showers, shaves, dresses behind our room's one locked door. I can't sleep once he starts stirring, but instead of moving, only think of moving: turning on the television, pulling back the drapes, picking up the snack-cake wrappers and placing them in the trash bin. Lisa, still unconscious, drools on both our pillows. And Leeanne, still too young to realize this is not the way it is supposed to be.

And before, only scraps of memories: a rainbow-painted bridge at the preschool half a block from our raised ranch house in Iowa, falling from the jungle gym in our backyard, a trip to the hospital to sew together my wide-split nose, Mom riding in the wheelchair, too woozy to stand, the needle, the thread; my first boyfriend, Chucky McConaughey, who broke my heart when he picked another girl to be his wife in Farmer in the Dell; riding the wrong bus home from school, the last one left alone, the driver calling in to dispatch, making a special trip to my subdivision; wandering off from my parents and getting lost in the mall. Leeanne was just a baby then, sleeping in the umbrella stroller as my father ran down the aisles shouting my name.

This morning, she's nearly four, but with the same round baby-face and wide-set teeth. Her swimsuit is too small—her colorless buttcheeks hanging out the back—but she puts on her goggles and waterwings anyway each afternoon at the hotel pool. Lisa comes, too, though she mostly refuses to swim.

And then we were climbing out of the station wagon, standing on a grassy hill overlooking seventy-three acres of farmable land. To the south: our jungle gym, magically transported from Iowa. To the west:

an enormous corrugated metal barn, home to owls and bats and mice and at least two litters of kittens every spring, birth-wet and mewing between the hay bales. To the east: the forest, dark and mysterious.

In the fluorescent-lit hallway of the school cafeteria, my mother signs a stack of papers. The school attendant asks my name, spells it incorrectly. The bus picks us up at the end of our gravel driveway on the first day.

1955

In the house on the top of the hill a single lightbulb sways from a socket in the middle of the kitchen ceiling. Water warms in kettles on the range. Steam rises from the galvanized tub* near the pot-belly stove, collects as fog on the windows, freezes almost instantly. Outside, birds have abandoned their nests, a few migrating to the barn, where cows huddle together with other cows, their hides now grown dull in the short winter days, sheep huddling with sheep, slow-breathing clouds of sheep. The fields, where nothing at all grows, lie dormant under layers of ice and snow, a luminescent sea broken only by the crests of brush and bramble, and the road, which does in fact lead here, and further beyond, though nothing now marks it but drift upon drift upon drift across the miles between the houses and right up to the outer walls, which do not block the wind but make it howl at least as loud as the three half-clothed children huddling under the patchwork quilt, waiting for a turn to bathe. Wilda pours a last kettle-ful of water into the tub, pulls Barry from under the quilt, wraps him in steam as he shivers into the bath, the water rippling around him, re-leases a bar of white soap from its crisp paper wrapper, myrrh and al-oes and cassia floating over acre upon acre of dormant land, over the stillness of his body under the swaying light, even over his dreams, which float beyond the drifts.

on the other hand . . . .

The silence can't be broken. Or it can be broken, but not by asking questions. Not by asking them again in a different way. Not by telling stories about galvanized tubs, or blackberries growing wild along the fence line, or a bridge in the forest made entirely of fallen trees. But then again, if the silence is held too long in the mouth, it might mean this is the muddy river's end, winding down the carcass of history to stop short of the delta—not dammed by a wall of silt, but disappeared like the rabbit into a hat, a puddle on the blacktop: evaporated. From the dense prairie grass to the dead truck coming for the milk cow to the cud still steaming in her mouth, there is a slow decaying—slow like Sunday driving, like the slab of meat roasting in the oven back home while the white-haired man rolls the windows down and puts his arm around his wife. Not like the interstate. The HOV lane. The constant spark of an electric grid. If you take away the wind in her hair, the potatoes and carrots becoming tender, the grass that grows and drowns along the river, what's left is called the *Dissected Till Plains*. And even that you've given us. *Corn Belt. Bible Belt. Belt made of leather and grain.* Nothing I can say will unbuckle us from this. Take away the river, too, and what's left is a field of dust. A hole that swallows light and sound can't produce a word that means both *Lie down in my green pasture,* and *Take me when you leave.* A vacuum to pass through. A void to fly over. A fly that lays eggs in the milk cow's carcass. I said the silence can't be broken. Neither can the telephone poles approaching from the distance. And then there is also the distance, which is not without its own history, its subsequent disappearance. Silence made visible. A tree growing up around the barbed wire fence, swallowing it rust and all.

1955

Bicycles in the truck bed, blankets in the steamer trunk, clothes divided evenly into each of four leather suitcases. He'll make a second trip for the toys and dishes. Those things can wait. Spotting the auctioneer walking across the lawn to shake his hand, Harold turns back to the truck bed, begins tying down the bicycles with a knotted length of baler twine. *I reckon it'll go pretty fast*, the auctioneer says. *Mmph*, Harold replies. The auctioneer doesn't press, has no words of consolation, wouldn't offer them if he did. Leave that to the ministers and morticians. Striding back toward the house, the auctioneer pulls a Pall Mall out of his shirt pocket, fits it between his lips, flicks the spent match in the general direction of the road, past the shade tree, where Judy burrows in the dirt with the sharp end of a stick. She keeps out of the way, but every once in a while she'll look up to see her father wrestling another chair into the truck, tying it down with a loose end of rope, wiping his forehead with the red handkerchief he keeps in his right pocket. His face tells her nothing. If he catches her looking, he'll curse or kick the dust in her direction.

When Harold hears the auctioneer begin calling for bids, he closes the truck bed and starts the engine. The dust mushrooms down the road long after he's gone. He comes back when the auction is over, the truck bed empty. *It went real fast*, the auctioneer tells him, handing him a thin envelope.

A man Judy doesn't know drives her father's tractor past where she still sits under the tree, tips his hat to her, turns the tractor down the road. Other men load the last of her father's belongings into wagons, old milk trucks, rickety pickup beds. Harold places another steamer trunk in the grass beside the truck, goes back into the house for a box of white dishes. Judy can't take her eyes off his face: clean wet tracks plowing through the fields of dust and dirt.

same joke . . . .

What else can he do but walk now to the barbershop, where there is only one barber standing at the window in his white jacket, or dozing in his leather chair, or sharpening his blade. He settles down for a close cut and a clean shave. *The usual*, he says. As in the story that begins: he stands for a while with his left hand in his pocket, fumbling loose change, his right-hand fingers twisting the toothpick between his teeth. Still a little buzzed from the whiskey. Says, *All the women have gone crazy*. All over town they're leaving their houses, straight off their porches into the street, down the cracked and heaving sidewalks, faster and faster, though the ground opens up to swallow them, though their husbands follow behind saying *Stop*, and they don't come home until the sun sets, until the street lights flicker and hum. Go anywhere, you'll see the silhouettes of their bodies wagging through town, dragging a woman-sized chair up to a woman-sized desk, their tiny fingers tapping at well-oiled keys, twiddling half a pencil while they wait to take your order, frozen that way for hours, until at last the weight must shift to the other foot, the head tilting to the other side. *It's the beginning of the end*, the barber says. *Mark my words. At first*, the man says, *it's a little pocket money she wants*. New drapes for the kitchen. A rug for the living room floor. Next thing you know she's balancing the checkbook while you warm up her car in the garage. Then she hands you the down payment for a house. Says, *Let me give you what we need.**

2006

It occurs to me, not for the first time, that my grandmother may be losing her mind. More and more, she starts crying on the phone for no reason. If I ask why she's crying, she denies that she is crying. It's been years since I've spent any real time in her house, and now that we're here, she asks me every few minutes if I need something to drink. She spends a lot of time staring off into space. She tells me, for the second time today, about the gristle the doctors found in her head, laughing for a moment at the thought of it, then goes silent again. After lunch, my grandfather takes my husband out to the shop behind the house. Grandma shows me around her garden, naming every flower, every bush, pointing out every ornamental orb and bird feeder she owns. She pauses now and then to ask again about the baby, whether we know yet if it's a boy or a girl, as if something in the action or the object prompts her: the bright red nectar in a hummingbird feeder, the smooth face of a stepping stone, the dusty boot box of photographs she pulls down from a bedroom closet. In her mind, each photograph is of my sister—my mother riding a mechanical horse outside Woolworth's, a great aunt I've never met—*Here's a good one of Lisa*, she says. She looks for a long time at the photographs of herself. In one she's standing in front of the cattle barn—her jeans rolled up to her calves, her hands thrust into her back pockets—squinting through her thick horn-rimmed glasses into the sun. She's seventeen. In another, she holds her two young children on her lap—my mother, maybe four; my uncle Kirk, still an infant—while under the pile of them all, my grandfather talks on the phone. *Here's my senior picture*, she says, and shows me another tiny rectangle: *Class of '47. I was in the school play.* I'm surprised by this bit of information, since I've always thought of her as being so internal, so reserved. Not shy, exactly. But withholding. Private. *Not a lot of lines*, she says, still holding on to the picture, *An extra, you might say. A bit part.* She returns the photograph to the box, without giving it to me, starts to get out of her chair. *But it's the extras who get the most time on stage*, she says, heading toward the kitchen, *already on when the curtains open. Haven't yet left when they close.*

1960

Every morning goes like this: Judy wakes up, eats a half-burnt piece of thin-buttered toast, and walks two miles to meet the school bus by herself. She walks so slow across the one-lane bridge and scoots rocks off the side with the toe of her boot, stopping to lean clear over the edge—far enough to fall—and sees herself reflected in the slow-moving creek. She spits into the mosquito nests at the water's edge and watches the larvae squirm and sprawl.

On the bus she pushes a boy out of his seat, gives another a bloody nose. He complains to the teacher while the children hang their jackets near the schoolroom door; she sends Judy to the very last seat in the very back row. Hours pass as she darkens the margins of her schoolbooks with the blunt end of a pencil, the day's lesson falling just short of her attention.

That afternoon, she wanders off the road toward a rusted-out car somebody's left sitting out behind the barn. She drops her books at the tire's muddy edge while she tinkers under the hood, pulling hoses out of their clamps, unscrewing every bolt, then puts it back together again. Each piece returned to its place, she plays like she has girl-friends and they all sing to the radio and go driving into town. The whole car's crawling with spiders and bees, but Judy fights them off because she enjoys this game more than she is scared.

Back at the house, she finds her mother in the backyard washing laundry, a chore that's kept her busy since just after breakfast. Judy offers to help, inching closer and closer to the big round washing tub, its sputtering agitator, watching the automatic ringer squeeze the water out. As her mother loads a basket to hang on the line, Judy reaches her hand toward the ringer. Laura swats her away—her hand, her butt, her face—all the excuse Judy needs to grab her fishing pole from the shed and head toward the pond.

It's not something her mother feels sorry for. Worrying and feeling sorry are not things her people tend to do. Except she knows sometimes Judy walks back on that road when it's raining so bad her rubber boots stick in the mud and no matter how cool the air she'll take them off and come barefoot the rest of the way. And every once in a while she plays sick so the bus driver will feel sorry and bring her clear back home. When he asks where she lives, Judy calls it Lemons,* even though it's really just a corner on the side of the road.

1961

Barry knows that between the house and the chicken coop lay a pot of geraniums, a thunderclap, a litter of kittens curled together like cooked beans in an empty barrel, a vegetable garden, green beans flowering, tomato vines flowering, a fragrance unmistakable even from the dusty gravel drive laid between the road and the entrance to the cattle pasture—the wide-swinging gate, and beyond: the tire paths fading in the waist-high grass, visible again only on each of the creek's two faraway banks—a clothesline tied taut to the stump of a sycamore tree, a wicker basket of clothespins, the tractor, its engine still ticking; a bolt of lightning, an aluminum silo, not quite shimmering in the moonlight, casting the same dull shadow whether empty or full, the loader chute, its planks bowing with mold and mildew, dry rot, wet rot, the ghost of a cow herded to slaughter, the ghost of its lowing still echoing from the trailer's closed doors, the crunch of feed grain under foot, knuckle bones, locust husks, a beehive buzzing in the branches of the mulberry tree: music that never sleeps but grows only more or less angry, more or less threatening; the shadow of an owl stretching and taking off from the barn, fox tracks in the mud, raindrops in the mud, a metal latch on the chicken coop door, the rush of ammonia, soiled hay, feather fibers in the air, the chickens hunched and tucked or drawn into themselves, their snores such an affable puttering—the downpour does not stir them—and the eggs, warm and solid in his hands.

rural route one

You and your sisters have always got on real good together. On hot summer days your sister packs peanut-butter sandwiches in a napkin she ties to your belt loop and you spend all day wandering the woods along the farm. Your daddy cuts a path with the brush hog and builds a square fort with sixteen knotty black logs instead of dragging them up to the house for firewood. You stop there every day to eat your lunch and you go skinny-dipping in the creek and splash your little sister with the cold cold water and sometimes she tells your daddy and all three of you get spanked. Sometimes at night your sister comes to sleep in your bed and you stay up late talking real soft together with your heads under the covers like two peas in a pod and your daddy has to get on you for staying up past your bedtime. One night after Mama and Daddy are in bed your sister tells you she's moving to an APARTMENT above the five-and-dime downtown and you pull the covers back to see her face in the dark and she says you can come to her place to see her anytime you like. The next day she takes all of her clothes out of her closet and packs them up in a big black trash bag and carries them over her shoulder out the door. Your mama and daddy holler real loud when they find out your sister is living in sin with a black man and you don't get to see her for some time.

a slur

A slur that no one ever says out loud. Not to me anyway. Instead: *one of those*. One of ours with *one of them*. They can't believe it. Degenerate, they mean. Filthy. Poor. Disrespectful. Which describes no one I know. The girl in my English class wears her hair in tight, neat braids, raises her hand and always gives the right answer. *Such supine poverty exists there.** Her skin is smooth and smells like lavender. My mother says her family took out a second mortgage on their house. *The other side of the tracks.* I should know better than to be her friend. My father tries to explain: *I'd shake one's hand. I'd even take blood from one.* He says this slowly, carefully, his eyes unblinking and intent, his hands resting on the arms of his chair, his feet planted firmly on the floor. *I just don't want one marrying my daughter.* Loud-mouthed, he means. Godless. Promiscuous. Illegitimate. Leech. But he doesn't say it, not to me. Failure. Wretched. Danger. Scourge. Instead, my mother says, *Disowned. Disappointment. Disaster.* Low-class, she means. Vulgar. Ignorant. *Embarrassing*, she says in the kitchen, slamming cabinet doors, opening the refrigerator, rooting for nothing in particular.* *Seriously*, she says, turning on the faucet, her palms braced against either side of the sink. *What will everyone say? What will everyone think?*

random facts . . . .

Missourians disagree about whether their state should be clas-
sified as a southern state, or as the southernmost midwestern
state. This disparity partially stems from Missouri's having been settled by Tennesseans and Kentuckians, and also because of its status
as a slave state before the Civil War. Despite popular opinion, however, Missouri was sharply divided on the issue of slavery: most of
the state south of the Missouri River had a strong pro-Confederate,
slave-owning contingent, but the area north of the Missouri River sat
too close to Iowa, a free state, for slavery to be profitable. Instead of
slaves, farmers in northern Missouri had large families, the women
and children laboring alongside the men.

. . . . .

My father's brother's wife's sister—a woman we'll call my cousins'
aunt—owns several Bed and Breakfasts in Macon, Missouri, one
of which is St. Agnes Hall. The home, built in 1846 by James Ter-
rill on land purchased from the State of Missouri, was used by the
Union Army headquarters during the Civil War. Every summer,
my cousins would come to town to visit their aunt, and would in-
vite my sisters and me to the house, where we'd play hide-and-seek
among the many bedrooms. Between the kitchen and the dining
room, a hidden doorway opened to a secret staircase leading to the
attic. In a concealed corner of the basement, one whole wall stood
gaping open: a long-collapsed tunnel, which some said led out of
town. In English class earlier that year we'd read *Uncle Tom's Cabin*,
so I knew about the Underground Railroad, and my cousin and
I would pretend to be runaway slaves, our older sisters hot on our
tails, ready to drag us kicking and screaming back to the plantation.

Thinking of that now, my cheeks grow hot, my hair stands up on end.

. . . . .

Between the 1830s and the 1860s, a population boom brought to Missouri many recent Irish and German immigrants, who, having fled famine, oppression, and political upheaval in their own countries, were not sympathetic to slavery. As of the 2000 census, German and Irish made up the majority of Missouri's ethnic population, with "American" coming in at a close third. "American" includes those reported as Native American or African American, but also European immigrants whose ancestors have lived in the United States so long that their descendants have lost track of where they came from.

. . . . .

In 1847, an ordinance banning the education of blacks and mulattoes was enacted in Missouri. Anyone caught teaching a black or mulatto person, slave or free, was to be fined five hundred dollars and serve six months in jail. A few decades later, it became illegal in Schuyler County, Missouri, for any person of color to be out after dark. Rumor has it, this law is still in place.

. . . . .

In *How the Irish Became White*, the scholar Noel Ignatiev describes how Irish immigrants, who were not initially regarded as white by native-born Americans of Anglo-Saxon descent, gained access to white privilege by distancing themselves from free blacks through racial violence and support of slavery. What Ignatiev does not say, however, is that even in a place with little racial diversity, people tend to invent subcategories of racial difference, which include not only physical characteristics, but also behaviors and attitudes.

. . . . .

Slurs used to denigrate poor whites include at least the following: appleknocker, backwoodsman, barn folk, barnyard savage, boondocker, broncobuster, brush hog, brush Yankee, bushman, bushwhacker, cedar savage, cletus, clodbuster, clodhopper, cornhusker, country bumpkin, country cousin, country folk, cracker, gawk, gook, ike, jack, jake, jig, jigger, lunk, country punkin, cowhand, dirt eater, farm boy, goof, hayseed, hayshaker, hick, hillbilly, honky, honyocker, hoosier, jackfish, jackpine, jayhawk, jiggerboo, landsucker, mossback, mudsill, oaf, old-timer, podunker, puddle-jumper, pumpkin husker, rabbit choker, rail-splitter, redneck, river rat, rube, sand-hiller, shacker, shotgun farmer, slue foot, sodbuster, stubble jumper, tiehack, timber rat, white trash, woodsman, wood tick, yahoo, yokel.

. . . . .

We are not that.

. . . . .

Whiteness scholar Matt Wray has argued that such labels are "stigma-types — stigmatizing boundary terms that simultaneously denote and enact cultural and cognitive divides between in-groups and out-groups, between acceptable and unacceptable identities, between proper and improper behaviors. They create categories of status and prestige, explicitly, through labeling and naming, and implicitly, through invidious comparison." It's the same old story repeated and repeated in all narratives about the One and the Other: "*cracker* has meaning in part because there exists another, unnamed, unmarked class: non-*cracker*."

. . . . .

It wasn't until I was in my midtwenties that I made my first black friend, a teacher and poet at least a decade older than me, and whom I greatly admired. One afternoon I tagged along as she went shopping, sitting on the floor outside the fitting room while she tried on designer dresses in Neiman Marcus, the salesclerks glaring at me. In Saks Fifth Avenue, I tried on a few things, too, including a seventy-dollar t-shirt I had no intention of buying, a luxury I could never afford. I think it was kindness that compelled her to buy it for me. Back in her three-story house, we sipped sparkling water and nibbled designer grapes: miniature delicacies that exploded on my tongue. We talked about our husbands, our writing, children. And then our conversation turned to race. She said, "You know, we can never start with a blank slate. You and I can never start from scratch." It wasn't out of the blue, but at the time I was bewildered, and soon after gathered my things and left. Only now have I begun to understand what she could have meant.

. . . . .

Missouri law considers drunkenness an "inalienable right." However, it is illegal to sit on the curb in any Missouri city and drink beer from a bucket.

. . . . .

Although black slaves coined the term "white trash" to describe white domestic servants, it was upper-class whites who appropriated and circulated the term as a vehicle for discrimination and prejudice against low-status whites, a way to flex and flaunt their social power, which they were not inclined to share.

. . . . .

Anytime I tried to leave the house wearing dark lipstick in high school, my mother would send me straight back to the bathroom to wash it off. *That makes you look trashy*, she'd say. Also: cut-off jean shorts, bleaching my hair too blond, letting my roots show, swearing, wearing a dirty t-shirt to the grocery store, wearing shoes without socks, wearing skirts without pantyhose, wearing pantyhose with runs, dirty fingernails, painted fingernails, chewed fingernails, mascara, eye shadow, overplucked eyebrows, underplucked eyebrows, dangly earrings, low-cut shirts, high-cut skirts, holding hands with a boy in public, staying out past ten o'clock even on the weekends, sitting too long on the front porch drinking a soda with my feet up, talking too loudly, standing on our street corner, sitting at the park watching boys play basketball, or even just watching the clouds.

1987

The breeder opens the horse trailer, lets the gate crash into the driveway—an echo trapped between the metal trailer and the metal barn—a cloud of dust exploding in every direction, several pieces of gravel tossed toward me and my sisters, standing well back in the yard. The breeder enters the shadow within, unties the loose nylon knot, says a few quiet words to the filly. And then, her ebony leg, slim and shining with sweat; her black tail, her auburn back, every muscle taut and twitching at flies, her long black lashes, her big black eyes, and inside: a deeper darkness that couldn't see us in the broad daylight, though we didn't know it yet.* I'm a little afraid of her: a little wild, still unbroken, her huge, heavy feet ready to crush me. The vet breaks the spell, reaches for the rope, ready to lead the horse into the barn to shoe her. But Mom gets there first—I don't even see her move from the place we have been standing—takes the rope in her hand, leads the horse around the yard a few laps—behind the house, out to the tree line, back to the barn—her hand running down the horse's neck, along her face, between her lips. I've never seen her show affection like this. We're all a little mystified. Leeanne sits down in the grass. Lisa jogs over to stroke the horse's other side. Dad signs a check, passes it to the breeder, shakes his outstretched hand.

1963

With the women occupied frying chicken in the kitchen, Judy can sneak out to the barn to see about the men. On any other afternoon, she'd let the back door of the rented two-story house slam to, but she knows that if her mother hears her dawdling about, she'll put her straight to work peeling potatoes over a metal pail on the porch. She holds the spring in her left hand—muffling its rusty twang—while opening the door with her right, wedging her body through the silent opening, then ushers the door back to its jamb before sliding barefoot into her new white sneakers, and darting off the steps. Halfway to the barn she bends to tie the laces, curses to see them already stained grass green. A few more steps and the grass path gives way to gravel and then to the smooth dirt path leading to the outbuildings, where the smell of pig shit hits her like a wall—*worst smell of all the animals**—and she takes a last fresh breath over her shoulder. This side of the barn, a patch of horseweeds stretching clear up to her shoulder blooms and sways as she passes, grows still again as she turns the corner to the cattle yard, where a fight has broken out, she thinks at first, but no: there is her uncle holding a rope, her grandfather tying it around the legs of a Black Angus bull, her father on its back, a sharp knife in his hand, at first clean and glinting and raised to the sun, then down and disappeared, the bull squealing like a pig, screaming like a baby, the men grunting directions, incomprehensible. Judy takes a few steps back toward the house, but doesn't turn. She can't look. Can't look away.

2006

At dinner the night after his interview, my dad tells me he wishes he'd talked more about helping to birth the baby sheep. *You can't be that close to life and death, hold a newborn lamb in your hands, and not believe in God.* Grandma Wilda says she wishes she'd talked less about Arthur, or at least been able to do the interview without Ralph in the room. *It just didn't feel right talking about my dead husband with the living one sitting right there beside me.* Grandpa Harold would have liked to talk more about his airplane. Grandma Laura wishes I had stayed in her house a night or two.

And then there are questions I'm told to avoid. My father's brother says something about *that whole thing with Joe.* I can tell from the context it has to do with losing money, but I press anyway. *What whole thing with Joe?* My uncle looks at me for a long time, sizing me up. *That's not up for discussion.* His face turns red as he says this, his blood pressure rising. His wife, my aunt, shifts uncomfortably in her seat. I leave it alone. Later I learn from my father what happened: No apology. No remorse. Now none of them can be in the same room.

After each interview is over, I wish I had asked more questions. Knowing these people so intimately made me hesitate. I know better, for example, than to ask my father's sister to talk about her son. The most she says is, *if he had lived.* As if his suicide were some kind of accident, the natural outcome of a terrible disease, a hazard of his tours of duty in Iraq. The point of these interviews is not to make my aunt uncomfortable. I am not a hard journalist seeking to expose her. It's not even been a year since he was buried.

I also know better than to ask my grandparents about losing the farm. I've already heard the story from Mom. Why make them tell it, too? How would it be different from the versions I've already heard?

My mom tells me her mother was beaten by her parents. I don't ask my grandmother whether this is true.

I also don't ask my parents to talk about racism. Or why they disowned my sister. I don't ask them to justify their actions to me. It's unjustifiable and we all know it. I don't ask about their marriage, or how and why it failed. I don't ask what anyone would have done differently. Instead, my grandparents look out the windows. My aunts and uncles buy us dinner. My father answers only the questions that I ask out loud. My mother breaks down in tears.

different joke

He tugs at the collar of his shirt, shaking loose the stray hairs sticking at his neck, glances at his watch before returning his hand to the change in his pocket—enough for coffee—and turns up the street toward the diner, where he has never actually eaten food, since it is not a restaurant exactly, but rather a crowded storefront where a collection of card tables wobbles under red-checked vinyl tablecloths, each table loaded with a plastic napkin dispenser, plastic salt and pepper shakers, plastic squeeze bottles of ketchup and mustard, and a black plastic ashtray, though there isn't a smoking section exactly, but rather men who smoke and men who do not smoke and they sit wherever they like. A waitress meets him at the table with a brown stoneware cup, which more or less matches the other cups in the diner, a pot of coffee in her hand, already pouring, a lit cigarette hanging out one corner of her mouth. *It's hot*, she says out the other. All day the coffee brews: Folgers in the pot with the brown lid and handle, Sanka in the pot with the orange, which no one ever drinks, but which the waitress brews all day anyway. All day she overhears their conversations: *the new minority*. Men move their families to town and work harder at collecting unemployment than finding a job. *Cuts to Social Security*. Meanwhile the house isn't worth the bricks it's built on. *Moving in the wrong direction*. She looks out the window through the smoke-stained curtains, between the dusty miniblinds. Outside: the town square, the courthouse, its green lawn shaded by an ancient oak tree. Inside, the men lean over their brown stoneware cups, gripping the handles a little tighter than before.

1964

Feathers fill the air in the garage, sticking to Judy's skin, the edges of her mouth, her hair. Her mother and her aunts haven't started yet, but instead stand in one corner tying their hair under handkerchiefs, tucking in their shirts, rolling up their sleeves. The chickens — ten or twelve fat hens — circle restlessly, scratching and pecking at the bare concrete floor, jumping into the air and flapping their wings. *Stupid birds don't know they can't fly.* The women give no signal that it's time to begin: one moment they've got their hands in their hair, the next moment the oldest sister turns and grabs a chicken by the neck, whips it around like a fast softball pitch, sends the headless body stunned and flapping a few feet before careening into the wall, then to the floor, where the flaps give way to twitches and at last grow still. And then the game is up: the other hens scratch and flap and claw at the windows and door: a way out, an escape. They won't escape until the smell of boiled chicken fat fills the air in the yard — a smell you can't wash off with Lava soap — as Judy dunks the headless bodies one by one into the pot of water boiling over the fire. She plucks the wet feathers out by handfuls, keeping her mouth closed the whole time, taking only a few shallow breaths through her nose — it's the only way she can keep from gagging on her tongue. The pile of bald chickens grows on the table beside her, their white feathers carried elsewhere by the wind.

1988

Whether or not the gray fabric of winter frays (gray bark becomes brown, gray limbs push green leaf buds toward each day's cold rain) two blue bird eggs lie cracked in the parking lot. The middle child pokes them with the branched end of a stick. No nest to return to. No brittle bird wings. No swallowing beak. Mostly discarded. Whether or not the preacher holds them down (blue water unbreathed, unswallowed; blue-painted pool, blue robes billowing: a sacrifice, a show) the two older daughters play a part. The oldest waves to her parents in the audience. The middle child tugs at the scratchy blue robe. *And the Father and the Son and the Holy Spirit.* Mostly sputtering. *Amen.* One goes back to the conference room and returns in her mother's blouse. Whether or not the other wears a white cotton dress (white plastic pearls nesting in their buttonholes, white half-unburied bone, white sugar pitched into the cracked white bowl). The youngest sleeps in the coatroom. Downstairs, the women are laughing. The men stand mostly apart. The middle child returns to the parking lot. Mostly dripping wet. Mostly wondering. A freight train passes, rumbles farther and farther away.

random facts

The official position of the Southern Baptist Convention is that the Bible is the infallible Word of God. Although church leaders admit it was written by men, they affirm that it represents God's divinely inspired revelation of Himself to man: *It has God for its author, salvation for its end, and truth, without any mixture of error, for its matter.* Any attempt to point out inconsistencies, errors, logical fallacies, or untruths is considered an insult to faith and a sin against God.

. . . . .

By the age of twelve, I had begun thinking I was Jesus. I told no one at first, because, ludicrous as it seemed, it was the only explanation I could imagine for the unique phenomenon of my existence. Later that same year, the pastor of our church was caught embezzling money from church donations. The deacons quietly dismissed him from his post, without any official explanation to the congregation. His youngest son took my older sister to the prom. When I confessed my privately held suspicions of my secret Godliness to my Sunday school teacher, she balked: *Why, that's impossible. Think of all your sins.*

. . . . .

Southern Baptists believe that a committed relationship between husband and wife should be modeled on the relationship between God and His people: a husband's love for his wife should mimic Christ's love for the church. He is responsible for the provision, protection, and leadership of his family. In return, his wife should graciously and respectfully submit to her husband as the church submits to Christ. It is her God-given responsibility to care for the home and the children, who should obey their parents without question.

. . . . .

In 1845, the Southern Baptist Convention became a denomination as a result of a disagreement with northern Baptists over the issue of slavery and white supremacy. The effects of that split continue to be felt: officially the SBC denounces racism; unofficially, many predominantly white congregations continue to deter nonwhites and mixed-race families from attending their services.

. . . . .

My family began attending the First Baptist Church when we moved to Macon, Missouri, in 1986. The week before, we had attended one service at the First Christian Church. I remember very little about that service, only the size and proportion of things: a cathedral-sized stained-glass mural behind the pulpit, my parents and older sister—enormous figures in the pew beside me—placing paper-thin communion wafers on their tongues, draining tiny shot glasses of grape juice. Not yet baptized, I couldn't take the sacrament, and cried enormous splashing tears until my mother, hoping to avoid a spectacle, let me lick the pulp from the bottom of her cup.

. . . . .

Southern Baptists observe only two ordinances of faith: communion and baptism. To become eligible for baptism, converts must have reached the age of accountability, and must accept Jesus Christ as their Lord and Savior. Baptism is considered valid only if it is performed by an ordained minister and occurs by complete immersion.

. . . . .

After my youngest sister moved out of the house, my parents stopped attending First Baptist Church and, soon after, divorced.

. . . . .

In a given year, more Southern Baptists attend Sunday school than formal worship service, which usually includes (in this order) hymns; prayer; performance by the choir, a soloist, or organist; the reading of Scripture; the collection of offerings; a sermon; and an invitation to respond to the sermon. Acceptable responses by members of the congregation include the decision to accept Jesus Christ as Lord and Savior and begin Christian discipleship, to enter into vocational ministry, to join the church, or to make some other public profession of faith.

. . . . .

Many Southern Baptist congregations hold separate Sunday school classes for girls and boys. Boys study the gospel, learning to follow the example of Christ's leadership, training to be responsible fathers and husbands and, sometimes, pastors and deacons of the church. Although Southern Baptists believe it is the duty and privilege of every Christian to make all people followers of Christ, girls are not permitted to enter the ministry. They are, however, allowed to make witness of their faith in other public ways: by joining the youth choir, by sharing the gospel with non-Christians, by memorizing passages of the Bible, by emulating the pious and servile wives and mothers of the Old and New Testaments.

. . . . .

As a rule, Southern Baptists oppose immoral vices: gambling, masturbation, homosexuality, tobacco use, alcohol, adultery, profanity, pornography, dancing, and sometimes secular music and movies. Many ultraconservative congregations also preach against television, materialism, magic as entertainment, any form of physical contact before marriage, literature, and romantic or platonic relationships with non-Christians or nonwhites.

. . . . .

Because I had been blessed with a good singing voice, I performed in the youth choir. Over the summer we toured on various mission trips: a week in Iowa, a week in Branson, a weekend in St. Louis. Fond of the spotlight, I performed most of our choir's solos and duets. "Amazing Grace" a cappella was undoubtedly my favorite, since each time I sang it—at Bible camp, at the seniors' center, in my grandmother's living room, for an audience of only myself—I brought my audience to tears. *Lovely as the white china sugarbowl,* I imagined them thinking. *Fine as the good silver spoons.*

2006

For those wishing to visit the Schuyler County Historical Society, there is very little about the two-story Victorian home where it resides along the southern limits of Lancaster, Missouri, that says *You're in the right place*. The building bears no sign, maintains no parking lot, and visitors who correctly identify the society only by matching its address to their directions park down the street before walking onto the dusty porch and knocking lightly on the outer door. If the society happens to be open, so is the inner door; if not, both doors are closed. The town itself operates in much this way. With a town population of roughly seven hundred (and getting smaller every year), Lancaster's one stand-alone restaurant recently closed, and the only place left to eat after church, my grandmother tells me, is the tavern, *which kind of defeats the purpose*. Located a few blocks south of the tavern, the historical society keeps no regular hours during its "open season," which lasts from roughly Memorial Day to the end of August, and does not maintain a website, email, or phone number. Part museum, part library, it does, however, maintain a dusty collection of old furniture, women's blouses, volumes of yellowed photographs, lace doilies, several collections of atlases, and a semicomplete record of the deaths and births occurring in Schuyler County between 1845, when the county was formed, and 1960.

My husband and I have come to the historical society because I'm looking for something specific. A man, actually. All I know about him is that he married a woman named Lavinia Johnson, fathered several of her children, was a farmer by occupation, and was probably born in North Carolina. He died, or had left his family, by 1850, which is when Lavinia and her children first appeared on the census in this area. Truthfully, I'd rather learn something about her—a woman running a farm on the frontier with only her children to help her—but without her husband's name, I can't track Lavinia back to North Carolina. No husband, no record. From what I know, her family was one of the first in Schuyler County—which was still part of Macon County at that time—but the Johnsons aren't listed in any of the historical archives as being one of the settling families. The 1840 census lists a Lavina Johnston living near Middlefork Township (a little over a hundred miles west of the current town of Lancaster), and a list of the "Pioneer Settlers" of Macon County between the years of 1833 and 1844 includes Enoch Johnson, Richard T. Johnson, Gabriel Johnson, and Jacob Johnson, any or none of whom might be the man I'm looking for. The census lists another family of Johnsons living nearby, all with birthplaces in North Carolina, like Lavinia. And that's where the evidence stops.

With a row of clouds gathering to the north, I leave my husband to peruse the atlases and head over to the public library to search through the microfilms. I realize before long that this is also futile, since the handwriting is mostly illegible. When I pick up my husband from the historical society, he tells me the old ladies have warned him they'll be closed again tomorrow. And now that it's nearing four o'clock, the town begins to shut down. People return to their houses and close the doors, shutter the blinds to the rain, and sit in front of their pedestal fans. In thirty minutes they'll be watching *Jeopardy!* My husband wants to head to the tavern for something to eat, but I'm ready to leave this dead end. Everyone's turning to ghosts.

1988

With Grandma Laura finishing up the dishes in the kitchen, the skeleton leans toward me, wants to know what the hell I think I'm doing in her house. My great-grandmother, I'm told, seems to me impossibly old, teetering in several directions on the verge of decay: the bones of her hands and feet bend crookedly under loose sacks of skin; the great mound of her belly bloating around her; a hacking cough that smells like death and peppermint candies. I get the distinct impression she doesn't really see me—one eye staring into the bridge of her nose, the other gone completely white—though she adjusts her glasses, sniffing in my direction. I don't answer, and she continues leaning toward me, frowning and expectant, until my grandmother returns to the room, drying her hands on a checkered dishtowel. *Get those children off the davenport*, she squawks. Grandma Laura and I look at one another, and then toward the couch: dozens of little pillows line the floral cushions, handsewn probably from scraps of old sheets and polyester dresses. She nods, and one by one I remove the musty pillows, place them in a neat pile on the floor. Grandma sits on a stool across from the old woman's recliner—I sit on the rug—asks her mother-in-law how she's been feeling. She wants her Vaseline,* a glass of tea, asks who put her pillows on the floor. I remember, suddenly, what my cousins told me at the last family reunion: *never used a bank, buried their money in the backyard or under the floorboards or something.* We spent that afternoon in a short-lived fantasy that our great-grandparents were secretly rich, and while the uncles were busy churning ice cream, we were digging behind the shed. But instead of jars full of money we found a geode, three nightcrawlers, the half-decomposed carcass of a barn cat. The old woman wants to go to the bathroom; we need to help her stand. Grandma Laura takes her right side; I take her left. She's heavier than I imagine, and we pull her up in pieces, each joint cracking as it separates. She cracks again sitting down on the toilet. My grandmother closes the door, shoots me a disapproving look.

With the old woman back in her chair, Grandma Laura heads to the kitchen to wash her hands. Before she turns the water on, the old woman has her breast out of her shirt — a giant, corpse-colored map of purple-green rivers — trying to nurse one of her pillows. I don't know where to look — the sagging, water-stained ceiling, the stack of broken televisions by the window, the knotted pattern of the rag rug on which I'm sitting. The whole thing is my fault somehow. I'll find the proof in either of their faces.

rural route one

Your daddy lets you drive his pickup truck on the gravel road to your house when he's real tired even if you're not old enough because he says it's something you need to know how to do. When you're driving he turns on the radio and listens to Paul Harvey.* Sometimes he disagrees with Paul Harvey and explains why instead of resting. Sometimes he listens with his eyes closed and his head leaned back against the window. You know he's worrying over money because when your daddy worries over money his forehead gets to looking like tilled soil, mounded in rows like the creek bottom. He works real hard on the farm but the soybeans aren't selling and neither is the corn and the fence needs repairs and the plow's all busted so you take the truck into town without asking and you apply for a job at the fancy Wal-Mart but they don't call you to come in for an INTERVIEW. You apply six times and when they do call you pack peanut-butter sandwiches every day for lunch and every time you get a paycheck you put it in your daddy's bank and sometimes his eyes get to watering and you think he might be going soft. You save every penny you earn, but disappointment's what you get for dreaming because every penny ain't enough. Your daddy's a proud man and his eyes water the hardest you've ever seen when he signs the papers that sell the farm but this time you don't think it's because he's soft.

cast out

Tell me again about the time we became human, when our arms un-barked, unbranched, broke just a little from the long-held pose and a tide of groundwater became our soft, blonde fur. As though a nudge was all we needed. As though the nudge split us apart—sparked in you; in me flaked off like birch. Tell me again how it was morning and we alone could not sleep, our feet too cold, too suddenly uprooted. How it was raining, the percussive music tapping a subtle insult on our roof. Was it raining? We always knew it would be: the fog spilling over the leafy hilltops into our field, the slow-rumbling thunder of crashing into ourselves, our naked shadows, our ditches flooding to the brim, the morning ebbing over us, silence blanketing its wake. It's evening now, months later, and everyone looks different in the hive-light of prime-time TV. As if nothing they could say is true. Tell me again who decided you'd be the lookout and I'd dig a hole in the ground; you'd carry buckets and I would be always surprised. How we came to find ourselves living out of suitcases, each of us isolated by loss. Like seedlings unable to take root. Like foals in twin sinkholes, their twin unspeakable thoughts. Tell me again how we held hands as we walked to the end of the driveway, the land already growing wild without us, something tameable growing within.

1965 . . . .

Judy—freckle-faced, slightly sunburned—stands at the corner, both feet on the lowest slat, looking into the pen. To either side, twenty-nine eager-eyed kids, their faces sticky with cotton candy and lemonade, and their mothers fussing over tousled hair, dusty knees, their fathers looking away. Judy's own parents stand well back, under the shade of a young maple tree—Harold's hands in his pockets, toothpick in his mouth, Laura's arms crossed over her chest. At the other end of the pen, twenty wild Shetland ponies stamp and huff and shiver behind a metal gate. Quick-fingered banjo harmonies trickle across the fairgrounds from the bandstand, and slightly after, the lyrics: *O when the sun refuse to shine.* The audience gathers around the fence. Not just the parents now, but also Harold's landlord, an impossibly round man in suspenders, his red face glowing from behind his pipe, his twin blond daughters licking twin vanilla cones, standing up straight in their perfect pink dresses. Judy pushes a red curl out of her face and spits, hard, into the dirt just inside the pen—a damp hole forms and sinks out of sight. The announcer—Judy thinks he looks familiar—enters the pen and faces the audience to recite the rules. She doesn't need reminding: once the horn sounds, you got three minutes to get into the pen, get a harness on a pony, and drag it back across the line. *Ready?* The line of kids mounts the bottom rung of the fence. *Set?* Judy pushes her sleeves up around her elbows. Applause pours down from the bandstand. *Go!* The horn sounds and a wave of adolescent bodies crashes over the fence. Judy isn't the first into the pen, and by the time her feet hit the ground, a cloud of dust and knees and elbows swarms around her. A mane darts just out of her reach. A hoof comes down on the toe of her boot. The audience cheers as one boy is kicked in the chest and his parents pull him, heaving, from the pen. *He'll be fine,* the fat landlord says, a little too loudly, *just got the wind knocked out of him is all.* Judy spots a piebald gelding in the corner, its back to the chaos in the pen. She moves slow toward it, slides along its bow-bellied side. Says, *You're coming with me, pony, even if you are too little for me to ride.* She loses the halter in the struggle, and instead grabs him by the mane and drags him, fat cart-mule that he is, back across the line. It's just the kind of spectacle this audience wants to see. But when the dust clears, Judy spots only her father approaching the corner of the fence. *I'll pull the trailer around,* he says, drawing the toothpick out of his mouth, *but you can't keep him. After all, it isn't really our pasture.* Judy's not even listening. The banjos strum their final chord. The audience claps and cheers.

2006

My mother lights up when I ask her about learning to sew, straightens the rings on her fingers, stretches out her hands—as if both a little bored and surprised by them. Her sewing room, which she takes me to after the interview is over, can be described as a closely ordered chaos: a labyrinth of tiny drawers for each little bobbin and spool, every pattern she's ever owned—the beige tissue paper folded neatly back into the envelope and filed away in a private system only she can understand. Strewn about the floor: the rainbow-colored ends of sewing thread, nips of fabric, the clipped edges of frayed, sewn things. As long as I can remember, she's maintained this kind of space: an extra bedroom, the storage closet, an unused corner of the basement. Always it's been off-limits to me—the painted table stained with coffee rings, her needles haphazard in their pincushions, the orange Fiskar shears marked in her bold black letters: *NO*. She was eleven when she learned to sew, she tells me. Her mother taught a 4-H sewing class in the living room of their house and every week they'd have a different project: a gathered skirt with a waistband, a little short crop top hemmed with rickrack, a matching three-cornered scarf. *And all my stuff got blue ribbons at County*, she beams. *Even blue ribbons at State*. In high school, her parents couldn't afford the clothes she wanted, so she waited tables at the Tastee Freez, used her tips to buy fabric, made the clothes herself. I'm not at all surprised by this: I remember her making many of our clothes when I was a child, even when money wasn't tight—and not just our clothes, but also cabinets and tables, stained-glass lampshades, porcelain dolls, crotcheted blankets and placemats, knitted sweaters and socks, paintings (in acrylic, in oil, in watercolor; on wood, on canvas, on cloth), exquisitely detailed Santa figures—their clothes hand-sewn from real velvet, real leather, real fur. These days, she spends most of her time making bears—

intricately crafted collectors' items she sells at trade shows across the country, through her website, on eBay. *I've sent my bears to London, Australia, Hong Kong*, she tells me as I thumb through a stack of beading magazines on the floor beneath her sewing table. *Places I'll never see*, she says, a little absently. *Can't hardly even imagine.*

1964

When the house casts a shadow reaching clear across the driveway, Arthur turns the tractor back toward the barn. Barry and Bruce follow behind, stacking hay bales onto the flatbed trailer in neat ricks, while all around swarm stray bits of straw, some pieces long as a finger bone, some small as the dust specks stuck to their faces, dark and wet in the creases around their eyes, making them look, from a distance, like much older men. Though they grow exhausted from this work, their bodies do not show it — the last bale lifted and tossed onto the trailer in one smooth motion, same as the first. The boys clap their gloved hands together in the steps between each bale, forcing feeling back into their fingers. At the top of the hill, Barry runs ahead to open the wide-mouthed gate, closes it after the tractor passes through, pulls his gloves off and stuffs them in a rear pocket as Arthur backs the trailer into the barn, where the bales will stay for the night, sheltered from the promise of rain. In the morning, after breakfast, Arthur and his sons will come out to divide the bales — some they'll stack in the barn to save for the winter, some they'll drive into town and sell at the farm-and-feed store. But now it's nearly dinnertime — Wilda hums in the kitchen as she moves the roast and potatoes from the pans to clean, wide platters; Brenda hums along as she sets the table: white porcelain plates, tall glass tumblers brimming with fresh lemonade, the everyday silverware: fork on one side; on the other, a fresh cotton napkin, knife, spoon. Outside, the men take off their boots, drop them just inside the back door. It doesn't take them long to shower, dress, appear at the table in fresh collared shirts, their hair combed smartly to the side. Everyone sits, joins hands, bows their heads. *Our Father*, Arthur begins, *who art in heaven*. The men let the women carry tonight's conversation, let them refill the empty glasses, let them take the empty plates back to the kitchen. *Hallowed be thy name*. While the women dry the dishes, stack them in the cupboard, the men take their usual seats in the living room: Arthur in the recliner, Bruce in the armchair beside him, Barry with his feet propped on the couch. Tonight they're watching a rerun of *My Three Sons*. Something about this episode jolts Barry out of near-sleep: Steven Douglas, the aeronautical engineer. Steven Douglas in a tie and a nice white shirt. Steven Douglas in an air-conditioned office, a neighborhood with wide, paved streets. Steven Douglas does not haul hay and neither do his sons. His sons go to school and come home. They play with their friends and pet the family dog. *On earth as it is in heaven.* By the time the women finish with the dishes, push the chairs back toward the table, take their seats in the living room, the dream is fully formed in his mind.*

1992

In the dim light of the early morning hours, I hear my father approaching before I see him—his heavy footfalls coming down the stairs, his boxy silhouette turning the corner, stopping at the foot of my bed, a solid hand on my foot, his solid voice filling his throat, urging me to stand and dress. Last night I laid out my clothes, draping them over the footboard of my bed: long johns, jeans, flannel shirt, sweater. In the kitchen I eat a bowl of oatmeal, set the dish down quietly in the sink, open the door to the garage, where my father sips coffee from a thermal travel mug, staring out the window, his eyes fixed on the east tree line. Several coveralls hang from the wall on long, gray nails. I pull one down, closest to my size, pull my arms into its grimy sleeves. I find a stocking cap and a pair of winter work gloves in the pockets—stuffed there last year, no doubt—the smell like old sweat, salt, and unwashed hair, still tacky with evergreen sap. He slings one shotgun over his shoulder—his father's, he tells me every time—holds the other out to me, hesitates as I reach for it, meeting me first with his eyes, a look that does not smile, but threatens with all the gravity of this moment and those that might follow. I take the gun from him, check the safety, my skin growing hot, open the chambers—not loaded. We had practiced shooting clay pigeons the week before. I didn't hit a single one, the brittle discs shattering instead in the pasture, against a tree, each time the shotgun kicking the wind out of me, my shoulder sore all week. We walk in silence around the house to the kennel to loose the dog. He lets her run wild around the yard, making several frantic laps around the house, while he loads his gun and mine. The sun barely beginning to rise. With a whistle the dog comes darting back, stopping abruptly at my father's feet, sits, wags her tail, her breath still racing. She's looking for praise he will not give. Our breath makes clouds in the mist of the horse pasture, our feet breaking the brittle stalks of frozen grass, steam rising off the mounds of earth, the rich black dirt. My father walks behind me and to the left, the dog ahead of us both, her nose close to the ground, pulling up every few steps to perk her ears toward the slightest sound. The tips of my fingers go numb. The dog stops, pointing toward a brush pile. My father snaps his fingers to get my attention. I know to move slowly, raise the shotgun to my shoulder, square my eye to the barrel.* He gives the dog a signal and she flushes them out. I hear their wings before I see them: flapping, frantic. They're not looking for mercy.

moon blindness

When the day darkens for the first time, levies against the flood of light that flows through the vitreous, the eye does not see, but remembers seeing: ghostly apparitions like moonlit shadows. Like blood pulsing through the inside of a tight-closed lid, though the lid is open. Wide open and still the eye does not see. Like waking in the morning to a second and perpetual night. A door opened, not to a wide, wind-bent pasture, the tall grass undulating in wild turns, even the shortest stalks warmed by the sun, but to another door that will not open. What could flower at this threshold but fear? A hundred thousand hazards suddenly drop across the path—the slightest hole, an electric fence, the low-hanging branch of a dense-thorned tree. And then there are shadows even in the memory of sight, each distinct pebble under foot bleeding into formless smears, until the mind stops trying to sift them, clouds pooling in that unlit sphere, more like a moon now than an organ of the body, its twin hemispheres growing tranquil in their desolation, unreflective. Until even the dark clouds grow darker and stop moving.

1967

B̲arry turns the corner after the last headstone in the row and the mower sputters to a halt. *Damn. Out of gas.* He lets go of the brake bar and takes a rag from his back pocket, wipes the sweat from his forehead and face, looks over his morning's work. Three hours and only a fraction of the cemetery mowed. Hardly worth the twenty-five dollars. His younger sister, Brenda, crouches over a grave, clipping the tall grass around the crumbling headstones. Barry would be the first to admit clipping is the harder job, but he pays her only seven dollars of the twenty-five. *Wasn't fair,* he tells me, *but she was a girl and I was older and, well . . . that's the way it worked.* He stuffs the rag back in his pocket, pushes the mower against the fence, and walks between the headstones toward the church, where he's left the gas can on the lowest of the church's three stone steps. He lets the names roll over in his mind: Stice, Condin, Lake. His feet rustle the grass. Its echo, barely audible, makes the hair on the back of his neck stand up on end and quiver. His sister sits on a grave clipping grass. No one else is here. Just then, the ground beneath his foot gives way and he sinks into the earth up to his knee. Barry can't help but cry out like a girl. His sister comes running, the shears still in her hand. A terrible vision of her catching a toe on a headstone, tripping, impaled. Struggling to free his foot from the hollow grave, he yells at her to slow down. Her cheeks redden, and she obeys, but keeps walking toward him. She takes his arm, helps him out of the hole. He stands and dusts the dirt clods off his socks and feet, looks around as if nothing has happened. A bolt of lightning. Just enough time before the downpour hits to run for the mower, pull it and the gas can into the chapel, which has become more shed than place of worship: the identical feet of absent pews imprinted on the floorboards, spiderwebs in every cavity, an ancient bird nest in the rafters. Mice take cover under a brittle hymnal on the floor in one corner. Barry picks it up and thumbs through the pages, so water-damaged as to be unreadable. *Almighty*. The suggestion of a chord, a whole note. Another bolt of lightning and the window shatters. Rain blows in through the hole.

1967

Judy leans backward in her chair, balancing on its two back legs, while her younger brother, Kirk, lays the last section of her wavy hair over the ironing board, each red strand steaming as the iron passes over it, becoming hot and slick and straight. Kirk balances the iron on its end, pulls the cord from the outlet in the wall, as Judy straightens up and checks her reflection in the mirror. Two headlights pass over her shoulder: a Buick pulling into the driveway, honking twice. She tucks her hair behind her ears and darts out the door without a word, leaving her brother to put her things away.*

Judy's best friend, a stocky blonde also named Judy, hands Judy a lit cigarette before backing the car out of the driveway. Three turns and two stop signs get them downtown, where teenagers from Unionville and the surrounding towns gather to drive in circles, to park along the courthouse lawn and shout to one another from open windows. The square is no one's final destination, but rather the meeting point. Soon they will split up and head toward their private endeavors — racing over blacktop roads, fighting in abandoned parking lots, dry-humping in the backseat of a father's car at the drive-in. Finally, the two Judys spot the white Plymouth and pull into a parking spot alongside.

Just the Judys we've been looking for, says the teenage boy in the driver's seat. *Get in.*

The Plymouth pulls away from the square, out from under the courthouse lights, speeds away from town, down a gravel road, stopping briefly at a rickety bridge — where the teenage boy in the passenger seat climbs out of the car and disappears into the ditch, fishing a twelve-pack out of the ice-cold creekbed, returning quickly to direct the driver the final dusty mile to an abandoned farmhouse. The driver turns off the headlights as he steers the car into the driveway, the house clearly visible in the moonlight: thick with vines, leaning slightly to the north, a sapling pushing up through the sagging porch.

The driver kills the engine, which sputters and stalls before coughing to a halt. In the stunned silence, the passenger cracks open a beer, hands it to the driver, who turns to the Judys in the back seat: *Somebody's going to have to go through a window and let the rest of us in.*

I'll do it, Judy says, climbing out the door. The passenger hands her a flashlight.

She circles the house once, checking for unlocked windows. There's a broken one in the back. She takes off her sweater, wraps it around her arm and reaches through the shattered glass to undo the lock. The window slides open easily, and Judy climbs in head-first, onto the kitchen counter within. She pulls the flashlight out of her back pocket, dusts herself off, engages the switch. Most of these abandoned houses are left empty, the occupants taking with them everything they can carry, even, sometimes, the plumbing. This house lacked only people: dishes stacked neatly in the cupboards, silverware in the drawers, table linens folded on shelves near the stove. How long had the house been vacant? A year? Ten years? It's hard to tell: the houses go feral so quickly, are reclaimed by the landscape, teeter, sag, eventually return to the earth. Judy puts her sweater back on and walks down the long hallway from the kitchen, stepping over a root pushing up through the floorboards in the entryway, unlocks the front door; the others come tumbling in. The driver hands Judy a beer as he pushes past her: *Nice job, Webber.*

Upstairs, the Judys find a closet full of moth-eaten clothes, a wedding album in a mildewed box on a three-legged chair, a steamer chest full of lightly chewed children's toys—everything smelling a little wet, a little musty, a little dulled by a thin layer of dust. Judy rubs her eyes and turns to her red-headed friend: *This place gives me the creeps. Let's get another drink.*

The boys have brought down a mattress from one of the bedrooms upstairs; the Judys dust off a couple of dining chairs and pull them into the room. The passenger pulls a deck of cards from his coat pocket: *Anyone for a round of Spoons?* The game, as always, moves quickly at first, the loser of each hand forced to take a drink. It's not long before the blond Judy and the passenger are out of the game and sprawled out on the mattress, half out of their clothes, beer cans strewn around them. Judy and the driver don't bother finishing the game, but climb onto the free side of the mattress. It always goes like this: A little kissing. A little over-the-clothes. Swap around and repeat. Then someone gets up to pee. Sooner or later they're back in the car, teenagers again, driving back toward the square, everyone a little drunk, sitting a little closer together. Judy looks out the window: hay bales line each pasture's fence line. The moon shines brightly, the stars like pinpricks in the sky.

1989

Into the driveway comes the rumbling form of the blue and white Ford F-150, its grill already encrusted with the oozing exoskeletons of half-dead things, the species no longer recognizable, a cloud of dust arriving seconds later, continuing down the lawn long after the wheels have skidded to a halt in front of the barn. My father kills the engine, though it continues to whistle and whir after he's opened the door, the rusty hinge announcing his left bootfall on the dirt. He leaves the windows rolled down, the glass just barely visible between the slack black rubber lips, cracked and broken by decades under the sun. I'm just tall enough to see inside: the wide black seat splitting open, foam seeping from the open wounds, daylight leaking in through rust holes in the floor. *Solid as a rock.* He motions for me to check: the dashboard smooth under a layer of gritty dust, its gray-black stitching straight and even. A radio plays both AM and FM stations. I test each of the push-button stops, press my palm against the aluminum steering-wheel spinner, catch my sister's reflection in the oversized mirror: horrified. She'll be sixteen in a few weeks. *I had a truck a lot like this when I met your mom,* my father says, unapologetically, not exactly by way of explanation. I look toward the house, expecting to see her on the porch, her arms folded across her chest, her weight held over her right foot. But the porch is empty. She hasn't even come outside.

2006

My grandmother replaces the cap on a bottle of clear soda, returns the bottle to the lamp table beside her, and clears her throat before telling me it was 1965 when she read in the paper that a woman was offering painting classes in a nearby town. She told Arthur that's what she wanted for Christmas: tuition for the class, as well as all of the supplies. I can't imagine how he afforded it all on his postal worker salary: an easel, a palette, several palette knives, assorted stretched canvases, a bottle of linseed oil, hog-bristle brushes, a small collection of oil tubes, an art box to carry them in. And where would he have purchased them? *It's been such a blessing to me,* she tells me earnestly. *It gave me a personality — I'd always been my parents' daughter, my brother's sister, Arthur's wife, the kids' mom. Painting made me Wilda the artist.* Although she'd been a creative person as long as she could remember — having painted, drawn, and designed clothes her whole life — the classes, more than anything else, gave her a community of her own: women she's been painting with all this time. *Cheating husbands, dead husbands, dead babies. What haven't we been through in these forty years?*

I don't know for sure whether she's ever sold a painting. I can't imagine that's the point. Instead, she displays them proudly in every room of her home, paying to have each one framed. For years, all she painted were portraits: each of her eight grandchildren, her brother, mother, and father. I can see them so clearly: the portraits of me and my sisters hanging in a hallway of our parents' home. To my knowledge, she's never painted her own children or their spouses. She also refuses to paint her two husbands, and admits to me it's because she's afraid to try, afraid she could never get the eyes right from memory, as if she wouldn't be able to capture the light. *And light,* she tells me, *is the main thing.* Instead, she paints mainly landscapes and memories — *snapshots of life,* she explains. I own two of the landscapes already, which I call "Bend in the Road" and "Creek with Stones," but she insists we pick another painting to take back to Houston. *Pick any one you like.* None are off-limits. My favorite remains "Saturday Night Bath," which hangs on the north wall of her dining room, but to take this painting would inflict a kind of violence: a memory that doesn't belong to me. We settle on "Barn with Chickens."

1968

With her left hand, Judy rolls the window down. With her right she steers the Beetle around the square, turns up the volume on her radio—a Creedence song she's taken to: *I like the way you walk, I like the way you talk, Suzie Q*—adjusts the rearview mirror, tucks her red hair behind her ear. In the passenger seat, the other Judy tosses her cigarette out the window. *They're still following us,* she says. *Can't they take a hint?* There's nowhere to hide from these persistent Milan boys; it's safer to keep circling the courthouse—around and around—well lit, public. Judy elbows her friend in the ribs, says, *Hey, I know that guy, pull in there.* And Judy directs the car into the parking spot. Her friend opens the door, motioning for Judy to follow, and leans to the window of a rusted-out F-150. Farm truck. No doubt from Lancaster or Livonia by the smell of it. He's all right looking, Judy guesses, maybe eighteen. Sun-bleached hair. Blue eyes. A big, honest smile. The kind of boy, she thinks, a girl wants to protect. But he's not interested, won't even look in her direction. He's too busy talking to her friend. *Fool doesn't know she's already got a boyfriend.* But Judy looks better in a bathing suit. She was even asked to model in a promotional ad for Lake Thunderhead. Spent the day in her bikini on a pontoon boat with a whole team of photographers. The Milan boys circle around again, leaning out the windows of their Pontiac as they pass Judy's car. She walks around to the other side of the truck. Opens the door. Climbs in. The country boy gives her a wide, white-toothed grin. Holds it for a while, lets it fall, his eyebrows pulled slightly together, as if great gears are turning in his head. *What's your name?* he asks, real slow and intent, as if this is the most important question ever to pass between his lips. Judy looks around for the Pontiac, a little nervously, noticing how his fingernails scoot along the worried ditches of the steering wheel, how he cracks his knuckles in the crookedest way. *Does this thing run?* she wants to know. He gives her a knotted look. Her love will be blunt like this, pushy even. He starts the truck, grins. Doesn't yet know what to call her.

still life with paperback

Now she is seated under the fluorescent light turning pages, peering through a pair of reading glasses perched on the end of her nose, searching for a spot in the book that convinces her to keep reading. A stack of books on the table beside her: Encyclopedia of Physical Deformities, Long Ago on the Prairie, At High Noon He Drew His Gun. She tries not to discriminate on the basis of jacket copy, cover art, though she has come to accept she has no interest whatsoever in Bodice Ripper, Foreign Travel, or Poetry of Any Kind. The rows of waist-high bookshelves lining the center of the room house more videos than novels these days, and who knows where the old books go: not sold, not donated, no used-book store around for two hundred miles. Maybe burned in the winter as fuel, or more probably, molding in a damp heap in a garage or basement. *A shame*, she thinks, licking her finger, catching it on the corner of the thin, yellowed page. *There was no answer, and lying in the darkness and listening, eyes wide with wonder.* Or sometimes eyes narrow and discerning. Or sometimes gone nearly blind. The fingers stiff and arthritic. The feet stuffed into orthopedic socks stuffed into regular socks stuffed into the last pair of orthopedic shoes, now planted on the floor in front of her, now bearing her full weight as she stands, steadies, and crosses stiffly to the librarian behind the checkout desk, who stares at the cursor on her computer screen, eyes wide with wonder. She waits patiently for someone to ask for her library card, though she does not open her purse to offer it.

1968

Even before the rooster flaps up to the fence post and begins crowing, Barry rises out of bed, dresses with his eyes still closed, shuffles into the kitchen to make himself a pot of coffee and pack his lunch. He grabs his keys from the hook near the fridge and goes out to start the pickup truck, a mug of coffee in his hand. This early in the summer it's still cool in the morning, and he cleans off the windows while the engine runs. He sets his empty mug on the bottom step just inside the back door and climbs into the cab, lets out the clutch, and backs away from the house. On the way to Unionville he listens to 1090 AM, KAAY out of Little Rock, Arkansas,* before pulling into Judy's driveway. She's already out on the step, her purse over her shoulder. They don't talk much on the drive to Milan, their eyelids so heavy with sleep. Most days they don't even sit close enough to touch.

In the gravel parking lot of the FM Standard Foods plant, women shout to one another from their cars' open doors, flicking the ashes of their cigarettes, pulling on their hairnets, tucking in their curls. Barry and Judy separate toward their respective locker rooms, where each tosses a brown paper bag into an empty locker, taking note of the number on the door.

On the plant floor Barry's job is to process the turkeys. The birds have already been defeathered, but he gets to pull off the skin, rend the edible pieces with a butcher knife: breasts, legs, wings, thighs. He reaches his arm into the carcass and pulls out its guts: intestines, stomach, heart, lungs. On the other side of the giant blue-lit room, Judy runs what she calls the "gravy boat." It's her job to check each TV dinner as it comes down the line, give each piece of turkey a squirt of gravy, send it on to be cellophaned, sealed in a cardboard box.

At lunchtime most of the workers take their meals outside, sit on benches and smoke their cigarettes. By noon, the weather is pleasant. Barry's never smoked a cigarette in his life, though he enjoys the smell, and Judy quit just after meeting Barry last month. The smell makes her grumpy, so they take their lunches to the grassy edge of the parking lot and eat their soggy sandwiches in the shade of a tree.

There's no place to shower, or even wash up thoroughly at the end of the day, so Barry and Judy ride home in the pickup truck smelling like turkey carcass and gravy. They're slightly more talkative now, swapping stories about life on the farm: one with navy beans, the other with the *Wonderful World of Disney*, but they're also hungry and tired, and some days it's easier to watch the road and turn on the radio. Once or twice she scooches over and leans her head against his shoulder. He doesn't ask for anything more.

1969* . . . .

On March 2 at the First Baptist Church of Unionville at 2:00 p.m. Miss Judith Marlene Webber, daughter of Mr. and Mrs. Harold Webber of Unionville, became the bride of Mr. Barry William Johnson, son of Mr. and Mrs. Arthur Johnson of Livonia. Rev. Jerry Reece performed the double ring ceremony before an altar decorated with white carnations and pink roses.

Mrs. Marie Schick of Unionville played a medley of wedding music.

Preceding the bride to the altar was the bridesmaid, Miss Judy Probasco. Her floor-length dress was blue satin featuring a short jacket with short sleeves and a round neckline over a straight dress. The bride, given in marriage by her father, wore a floor-length dress of white chantilly lace and white satin bodice featuring bell lace sleeves and empire waist which was made by the bride. Her veil of silk illusion net was held by a large satin bow trimmed with pearls. Her bouquet was of pink baby roses and ferns.

Bruce Johnson, brother of the groom, served as best man, Kirk Webber, brother of the bride, served as usher. The groom and the best man wore white carnation boutonnieres.

For her daughter's wedding Mrs. Webber chose a three-piece suit of light pink with brown accessories. Mrs. Johnson, mother of the groom, was attired in a three-piece gray suit with black accessories. Both mothers wore a blue-trimmed carnation corsage.

The reception was held at the bride's home immediately following the ceremony. The table was covered with a white crocheted tablecloth with a blue underlay. The three-tier cake was blue, trimmed with white swans and pink roses and was topped with the traditional bride and groom.

Guests were served cake, mints, punch, and coffee by Miss Brenda Johnson, Mrs. Norma Dixon, and Mrs. Betty Fox.

Mrs. Johnson chose for travel a blue wool suit with black accessories.

They will make their home at Sunset Trailer Court in Columbia, Missouri.

witness

knock on the door, say, *Hi there*. Say, *Is Jesus Christ your Lord and Savior?* I forget to make conversation first. I forget the transitional sentences. I'm no good at improv; I need the script. *There are four things I want to share with you*, I say. Mnemonic devices. A nifty brochure. Look at my bracelet. Look at my smile, I think. You can't resist me. Let me take off my mittens. Let me open my coat, step inside your open door. It's so warm here already. Let me open my Bible. I've marked each page. *For God so loved the world. 3:16*. All have sinned. Now smudged. *And fall short of the glory of God. 3:23*. Please excuse me, you say politely, I've just put dinner on the table. But what good is dinner if you're burning in hell? Your flesh will bubble and char. Think of the smell. I'm getting desperate. Think of the children. What if this is your only chance to save them? Let me take off my sweater. Aren't you lost? Aren't you blowing like dust? The good news is this: Christ already died for you, already shed his blood on the cross for you. *Repent*, I say. *Or perish. 13:3*. Sins of the spirit. Sins of the flesh. Look how happy I am since Jesus took root in my heart. *Thank God*, I say, *for allowing His Son to die*. Thank God for raising him from the dead. Thanks for stopping by, you say. *Beg his forgiveness*, I say through the crack in the door. A veil of snow, the shrouded street. Promise Him you'll change. *Promise me*. The door closes, locks. Amen.

trespasses

i.

At the northeast corner of our farm, roughly a stone's throw away from the narrow gravel road that led past our house, stood an old, sap crusted evergreen tree. Nailed to its trunk a white sign with red letters read "Private Property / No Trespassing." This sign marked the border between our forest and the forest belonging to our neighbor, who didn't live on the property, and whom I had never met. The trees on our side of the line looked like the trees on his side of the line. Our underbrush like his underbrush. Because the border lacked a fence, birds and deer and rabbits crossed and recrossed it at will. I knew on which side of the border I belonged, but I crossed it anyway, entering a place where I was not welcome. (It thrilled me.) Anyone driving by on the gravel road would never know I didn't belong there.

ii.

In a recent comment thread on Facebook regarding an article I had posted about an author writing in a dialect associated with a racial group (not his own), a former classmate told me he finds all writing in dialect offensive, even if—to my surprise—the writer is writing in his/her own dialect. He explained:

> Part of the problem may be that we tend to associate dialect with class, and we presume that writers are educated, and of a means above that class. That is, the writer has become a member of a group more privileged (WE ALL HAVE SO MUCH MONEY RIGHT) and is therefore no longer a member of the socioeconomic group she or he claims to represent. Any representation of a group's speech patterns, to me, seems less than genuine.

I responded:

> Hmm. An interesting point. Though I think some of what offends me about dialect work is trying to mimic non-standard pronunciation on the page. Altering spelling to mimic speech and whatnot. (That bugs me to no end, and is why I still can't stand reading Mark Twain.) I find representations of non-standard grammar less offensive, though. Or if not non-standard grammar, at least regionalized syntax. I occasionally do that in my own work, and in doing so, sort of re-tune to a certain language already/still in my head. Getting educated didn't silence it, but rather taught me how/why that music was "wrong," which I now kind of resent.

iii.

During dinner, my husband asks what I've been working on. I try explaining how the term "white trash" is a racial slur. He puts down his scotch and raises his eyebrows.

For many whites, I say, whiteness is the invisible, unraced center of an otherwise racialized world. These same whites use the term "white trash" to differentiate between themselves and poor, low-status whites, and in doing so, inscribe differences that are not just social, but material, physical—visible on their skin, in their manners, morals, and behaviors—making "white trash" a marked, racial, and degraded form of whiteness.

He points his finger in my direction and interrupts: you should say that this is only the case in America. In South Africa, say, or China, the relations and the reality would be totally different.

I say, Thank you. I will consider mentioning that. I sip my wine and pause before speaking. The server comes to retrieve our empty plates, leaves a dessert menu by our elbows.

As I was saying: because they're marked as not quite white, "white trash" do not experience the same effects of white privilege as middle- and upper-class whites.

Not quite white?

Right, not quite white. Their skin is white, but the way other whites treat them is not.

iv.

Around the same time I took my first poetry workshop in college, I started changing my speech. I said "am not" instead of "ain't." "Should have" instead of "shoulda." I dropped "ma'am" altogether, and instead relied on "Doctor," "Professor," or "Ms." By the time I was accepted to graduate school and started teaching my first writing class, I'd gotten pretty fluent, though occasionally overcorrected when nervous or intoxicated. Because it wasn't a word I was used to saying, "not" was particularly troublesome and almost always came off sounding a little British. A lot of people must have noticed, but only one person ever gave me grief: a student of mine from an affluent suburb, who spent the whole semester coming to class late, interrupting me during discussion, turning in assignments a week after they were due, or not turning them in at all. During the midterm conference, I pointed out that his grade was suffering. He pointed out that his father was rich and his taxes paid my salary. On his end-of-semester evaluation, he wrote that I was an idiot and needed to drop my "affected accent." "Ms. Johnson," he went on to say, "has no business at this university or any other."

He was right, of course. Social norms and conventional wisdom dictate that white trash (or their variants: hillbillies, rednecks, and crackers) are incongruous with the college classroom, even more so with the lectern at the front of it. This symbolic divergence stems partially from the downward, degrading force on these cultural figurations of whiteness—stereotyped as thick-headed, ill-spoken, backwards, lazy, immoral, violent, and illiterate—and also from the upward, elevating force on the figurations of the academy itself—consider the ostensibly class- and race-neutral terms "academics," "intellectuals," and "artists"—in effect, building an invisible fence around any academic, intellectual, or creative enterprise, such work being the private property of a relative few.

In the years since that initial course—the one with the pain-in-the-ass student who tried to out me—I've become a fluent speaker of standard American English, though I tend to lapse into dialect when I go home for a visit. I've also changed my clothes and my teeth and my hair—a slow and gradual process. I cover my tattoos any time I need to be taken seriously. I own a house in an affluent suburb and teach writing at the university.

No one knows I don't belong here.

V.

And then there are the invisible lines of maps, which have no corresponding mark upon the ground, in the soil, through the trees or the grass or the air, though it is possible to cross them. To cross the line, to toe it, to pass over an unspoken but understood border. And then there are the visible borders of cities, which are not so much clear and definite lines of demarcation as intervals of either condensation or dissipation, depending on whether you are arriving or leaving.

And then there are the invisible differences among people, which have no corresponding mark upon the skin, in the hair, under the fingernails or eyelids or lips. But there are words they speak to one another, and then there are words they speak to you, the outsider, and the difference lies not so much in the words themselves, which mean very little when it comes right down to it, but in the history of people speaking to one another in that place, which you could not possibly know unless you happen to also be from there, in which case it doesn't need explaining.

vi.

The tricky thing about passing is that it only works when the passer is invisible. For that reason, passing only works in one direction. The passer cannot un-pass or pass back, since in the act of passing the passer becomes visible to those who recognize the truth. Maintaining invisibility can therefore become all-consuming—whole lives spent keeping up the ruse. For that reason, the benefits of passing must outweigh the effort and anxiety expended in pulling it off, or no one would do it. Certainly, the benefits vary for different individuals, but might include the thrill of getting one over on the dominant culture, access to power and privilege, invisibility itself, or the sheer joy of sticking it to the man.

Let's be clear, though: the benefits of passing never include real, structural change. Under no circumstances can passing be considered an act of subversion; in fact, passing actually reinforces systems of oppression that operate by bestowing unearned advantages on some and denying them to others. It is only through a kind of semiotic sleight of hand that the passer takes on the symbolic form of a privileged other: though the passer's actual, physical, material form remains the same, its signification changes. Passing does not, therefore, challenge or condemn those symbolic forms, or the advantages they bestow, or the structure of the system, or any individual who reaps its rewards. Instead, passing exploits an arbitrary relationship between a certain physical form and its symbolic signification.

Once we acknowledge the terms of this phenomenon, we find its manifestations abound. Consider the following: if we agree that a discrete social identity ("whiteness," for example) functions as a symbolic territory (it is finite, has boundaries), then we might also agree that any given literary genre (poetry, for example) occupies a similar sort of territory (it is also finite, has boundaries), in that language performs a sleight of hand in order to pass as "poem." One problem, then, with genre is that the mode and manner of our articulations are limited by the parameters of what will pass in that territory. Which raises some questions: What passes as poetry? What passes as nonfiction? Where is the border between verse and prose, fact and fiction? Who has drawn it? Who polices it? And according to what aesthetic?

vii.

One day in late spring I was sitting poolside with some of my friends from school. Some were drinking beers or chilled white wine. Several floated on inflatable rafts. I sat in a lounge chair—a wide scarf covering my pregnant belly, just beginning to swell—reading a trashy celebrity magazine and drinking Diet 7-Up from a plastic bottle. It was turning out to be a fantastic day. Near the grill, two of my fellow students began arguing—I couldn't help but overhear—about the sublime and the beautiful. One quoted Matthew Arnold. The other, Komunyakaa. I thought to myself, *for Christ's sake. It's fucking Saturday.*

Days later I was sitting on my bed, fans blowing on me from every direction. I had been reading who knows what—maybe student papers, maybe poems from workshop, maybe postcolonial theory or an Irish novel or any number of other things. The point is, one moment I was reading, and the next I was looking out the window, and then the words were already bubbling out of me and I didn't stop typing until they ran dry. I cried the whole time like some kind of blubbering idiot. And then there were my words. My real words—naked, visible, with all my linguistic imperfections laid bare.

Me. Mine. My own.

And for once I didn't try to revise the piece into something recognizable to my academic peers. Because although I've learned to correct the ways in which my native idiom is often ungrammatical, I've also learned that there's something about my experience growing up in a poor farming town in the Great Plains that gets lost in the translation to standardized academic verse. I've read that piece in public several times, and because I can't read it without falling back into my native pronunciation, with each reading I out myself: A hillbilly. A redneck. A white-trash class-passer.

No one tells me I don't belong here.

jackson street

You move into a white house with blue shutters and a yard with exactly thirteen trees on a paved street in town and your daddy tears down all the walls and puts up new ones because black mold spreads where you can't see. He works at the power plant and drops his yellow hard hat by the front door and your mama waits on rich folks at the restaurant and gets real dressed up for work every night and you don't have to set the table anymore because you and your sister eat peanut-butter sandwiches for dinner and watch cable television before you go to bed. Sometimes you cut the sandwiches into circles with the mouth of a glass and sometimes you add pink and white candy sprinkles Mama keeps in the cupboard for cupcakes and you tell your sister you've made her a SURPRISE. You walk to high school every day and you smoke cigarettes and cough down the peach schnapps your mama keeps hidden in the very back of the highest kitchen cabinet and even though it burns your stomach like hellfire you follow the kids to the one-block downtown and drive your truck in circles because it's the only thing to do. You make friends with a girl your same age and she lets you spend the night at her place sometimes and you sleep real soundly in the AIR CONDITIONING. Sometimes she sneaks her boyfriend in and they have sex in the bed right next to you. One night he brings his friend over and he kisses you and claws your clothes off and you just want to sleep but his breath is stale and sweet like the beer your daddy drinks and when you try to push him off and tell him to stop he puts a pillow over your face and jams himself right up inside you and you can hardly breathe it burns so bad but there is nothing God will do.

1992

My grandfather starts the engine—the single propeller shudders, jerks, begins spinning—then hands me the spare headset, motions for me to put it on. *Keep your hands to yourself,* his voice gruff as ever through the earphones. Outside, on the tarmac, our family huddles near the van: Dad snapping pictures with a new camera; Mom standing near my grandmother, Leeanne crossing her arms over her chest, kicking at a loose piece of asphalt. All day no one has mentioned Lisa, who is no longer welcome at Thanksgiving dinner at my grandparents' house. Grandpa orders me to help him with a few quick checks: Gas? Check. Seatbelts? Check. Wings? He turns to me, winks. Check. And then we're pulling away toward the end of the runway. We don't need to wait our turn—there are no other airplanes flying today, or any other day, from this runway. He revs the engine and we're hurtling toward the tree line, faster and faster, until the yoke between my legs lurches toward me. I almost reach for it. *Don't touch anything.* Faster and faster. And just like that we're off the ground— effortless, but for the engine's feeble roar. He rolls us southward, back toward town, and points out the landmarks he wants me to see: the house they own on Union Street, their several sets of storage buildings, the tractor shop (which went bankrupt), the restaurant they bought (which burned to the ground), the spot where he built a fireworks stand with his own two hands (now a bare stretch of highway); the farms they rented when Mom and my uncle were children. It all looks the same to me: asphalt shingles, anonymous rectangles at this height, surrounded by trees, divided by streets—all of it completely still—and beyond: the neat, dispersant geometry as far as I can see.

1973

It won't take long for Barry to pack his entire office. He pulls a file box down from the shelf on his way in, slams the door behind him. The blinds rattle against the window. No one looks up from their desks. Who knew this was coming? A petty thought, and he's immediately ashamed for thinking it. He pulls his framed diploma down from the wall, stuffs it into the box. Interoffice politics is what it boiled down to. A framed wedding picture on his desk. Mistakes were made and someone has to answer for them. A drawer full of pencils, sharpeners, paper clips. Barry's low man on the totem pole so it might as well be him. Calculator, graph paper, an unopened pack of chewing gum. On any other day, his eyes would well up with tears. He's always been so emotional, just like his father. But his mother called on Tuesday. She didn't make small talk, didn't beat around the bush. She came right out and said it: *Your father has melanoma.* Barry hasn't told Judy yet. She's so pregnant. He's not sure how she'd take the news. And how will he tell her this? Just now she's sitting in the wood rocker in a corner of the living room, knitting a sweater for the daughter they're expecting this fall. He pulls his jacket from the coat tree, hesitates for a moment while he decides whether to put it on. Looks outside: not raining. Throws the coat in the box with his other things, hoists it onto his hip as he reaches for the door. He won't cry over losing this job. Nothing could matter less.

1995

orgeous how the woodgrain of the dining table's polished surface reflects the light hanging over our heads, gorgeous my fingerprints like stepping stones toward the open textbook, an island at the center of some dark unmoving sea, gorgeous the equations my father etches into my notebook, the perfect and rational steps he pencils toward an unknown X, his free hand balled into a fist on his knee, like he's laying it to me straight, telling me like it is, but his voice is so quiet and slow and even—*don't you see?*—I don't see. But gorgeous the echo his voice does not make against the curtains, gorgeous the smell of the wind blowing in through the screen, stirring the pages of my book, stirring my mother out of her chair in her sewing room down the hallway, her shoes scuffing the hardwood, her hand on the knob of the door. And gorgeous the arc of the notebook my father now pushes toward me, the wake it does not leave in the dark polished sea, gorgeous the pencil, the white page, its lines never touching from here to infinity, the incalculable blankness between.

2006

For a long time he doesn't respond to my question. Instead, he sits very still. Completely still, in fact. In the way I've come to recognize means he is thinking very hard. When he does begin speaking, it's very slowly, choosing his words carefully, constructing them as if for the first time. As an inventor. As if from scratch. *I would want people to know*, he says, *that my father was my best friend.* He gestures with his left hand, occasionally bringing it down into a single-fingered point. Not at me, exactly, but as if to tap the word that he is saying. While with his other hand he shuffles and reshuffles a stack of photos he says he doesn't really want to tell me about. This is not to say he doesn't want me to see them. Instead he wants me to know that his father was honest and well liked. Also, he was an excellent quail shot. *He could go out with eight shots and come back with eight birds. Me, I'd shoot off a whole box and come back with maybe three birds.* His father was also good at bridge. Good at cards in general. Good at just about everything. *He won table tennis tournaments in Africa, don't you know.* My father had started playing against him in high school. Of course they kept score. When my father left for college, he played table tennis with his classmates, the other young men in his dorm. Arthur didn't play while Barry was away, but when Barry came home, they'd spend his entire visit in the basement, bouncing the ball back and forth between them. When my father moved to Tennessee for his first job, he played in table tennis leagues. But, again, Arthur wouldn't play while his son was away. *But I'd come home to visit and we'd play.* My father is crying now, and no longer talks slowly, but rushes headlong toward the end of every sentence, where he takes an enormous sobbing breath. I ask if he wants to stop for a moment. He says, *No, I'll get through it.* Just after I was born, when my parents were living in Muscatine, Iowa, my grandparents drove the three hours between our houses to visit. Arthur, my grandfather, who was exhausted from the treatments, was even more exhausted by the drive. But shortly after arriving, he asked my father for a match. *I beat him something like 21 to 18*, he says, his voice becoming increasingly difficult to hear. *We played another game, and he beat me. It was the last game we ever played.* Three weeks later my grandfather died in a hospital in Columbia, Missouri, nearly four and a half hours away.* *And that game before the last*, he says, *the one where I won*—he hangs his head for a moment, collects his voice, his breath—*that was the first time in my life I had ever beat him. Can you imagine?* Sheets of tears roll down his face. *And he was happy for me. Happy that I had finally won.* My father succumbs to the sobs, chokes, says, *Okay. Now I'll stop.*

liturgy . . . .

And all of God's Baptists say Amen. Say, Blessed be the name of the Lord. Say, the Lord is our strength, our portion, our shelter, our strong tower, our ever-present help. Say, Thank you, Lord, for shining your light on my life. Thank you for your blessings: the roof over my head, the car I drive, the health of my children, my wife. Say, Thank you, Lord, for the valleys you place in my path, the difficulties I face, thank you for trying to shape me into the image of Your Son. The Bible says that your wrath was poured out on Him at the cross. And if we are found in faith to believe that salvation, we will not face your condemnation. If we are under the blood of the Lamb, if we have placed our faith in Him, we should not fear your wrath. Thank you, O Lamb of God. Amen and Amen. Paul the Apostle says, "In everything give thanks." As in: Thank you, God Almighty, for the hurt, for the sorrow, for the difficulty, for the doctor who says my father is dying. As in: give thanks. Romans tells us that God is working all things to the good of those who love him and are called according to his purpose. God has a plan for us and his plan has never been sidetracked. He is sovereign and in control. Thank you, Ruler of the Ages. Amen and Amen. When Job's farm, his livestock, his servants, his home, and his children were destroyed, he rose up, tore his robes, shaved his head, fell to the ground in worship and said, "Naked I came from my mother's womb and naked I shall return. The Lord gave and the Lord has taken away. Blessed be the name of the Lord." And all of God's Baptists say Amen. Say, yes, God is holy when life falls apart. God is good. Is gracious and merciful. Nothing about God changes when our meager circumstances do. Nothing, I tell you. And all of God's Baptists say, Thank you, Lord Our God. Because we have His promise: "And He will call His children to Himself and those who are alive and are left will meet in the clouds. And we will be forever with the Lord."

1978

He thanks the minister for calling again, places the telephone back on the receiver. So dizzying: the spiral cord, the chaos of its occasional kinks and knots, twisting and untwisting around and down itself, wrapping and tangling in its upward-tending half. When was the last time he spoke to his father on the phone? It was brief. Always brief and with some mundane purpose: *How is the family? How's your game?* The same conversation over and over. What had they ever really said to one another?

He can't decide where to direct his eyes. To the east, beyond where the table sags under the weight of churchwomen's casseroles, beyond where his wife sits to nurse their infant daughter, four walnut feet prop his mother's easel sturdily in the corner. Months have passed since she's picked up a brush, and with each passing day it becomes harder to think of her making even the slightest mark. To the west: the fringe of the bedroom rug, a chest of drawers, the sheen on each pair of his dark socks, each dull gray undershirt, the well-worn ditch where he slept on his right side, facing westward, all these years.

Instead, he marches straight north out the door, the screen slapping to behind him. Three squirrels bolt from the lawn. All the dandelions have turned white: like cotton balls, like baby sheep. Even fully shaded from the bleaching rays of the midday sun, the porch lumber has faded. The color still on his father's hands long after he'd stained it.

Seed tufts dance on a cool breeze off the pasture. One finds the slightest splinter and catches there. He pokes it with the blunt end of his finger. An abandoned sparrow nest rustles in the rafter overhead. And farther: the tree line, the long-vacant silo, the algae-slick pond.

All of it bought decades ago for the sole purpose of raising children, now grown, raising children of their own. The driveway will need to be regraveled, he thinks, the grass mown, the truck sold. The deep lines in his palms will grow deeper. The house will continue facing north until it's gone.

prodigal daughter* . . . .

The first time I get drunk I'm fourteen, riding in the back seat of a car next to my friend Lauren. It's after midnight, a blacktop road outside the city limits. We're trying to find "Airplane Hill," a stretch of a hilly farm road straight enough to build up some speed and launch a car, however briefly, into space. In the front seats two boys from Kirksville pour Everclear* into a couple of Cherry Limeades, take turns pushing cassettes into the tape deck: Boys II Men, Bobby Brown, Billy Ray. The four of us empty the bottle and two packs of cigarettes before we find the spot. We take turns driving, each of us pushing the gas pedal closer to the floor, the speedometer inching toward infinity: 75, 83, 97, 104. I drive the car off the shoulder, put my cigarette out on my knee. We all climb out, stumble down the road, pull the hubcaps out of the ditch.

. . . . .

A month later Lauren and I are caught shoplifting at the mall. The sales attendant sees us stuffing t-shirts into our bags, pulls us into the office, calls the mall police. While we're waiting, I ask to use the bathroom, where I flush several sets of earrings and a bracelet down the toilet, stuff a necklace into the trash. We're hours away from home; my mom on the other side of the mall, buying school clothes for Lee-anne. Without any evidence, the police don't arrest us, and we are released on the condition that we meet with the juvenile officer back home. A week later I tell the whole story in her office: *I don't understand*, my wide eyes watering. *Stealing is a sin.*

In July, Lauren and I sneak out of her house and spend a whole night with a can of spray paint, leaving the words *Fuck You* on sidewalks, under bridges, the backsides of abandoned buildings.

That August, I'm caught smoking in the school parking lot when I'm supposed to be at an FBLA meeting. The psychology teacher knocks on my window, asks where I'm supposed to be. I blow smoke into his face. Two weeks of Saturday detentions. A week later, I ask too many questions in chemistry: *Why do we need to know this? When could we possibly use this information? Who actually cares?* The teacher keeps me after class, gives me a piece of his mind: *Never in my life. Won't amount to anything. Barefoot and pregnant. Poor white trash.* He wants to know if he's been clear. *Crystal*, I say. A month of Saturday detentions. A week later, I'm caught drinking before a football game. I hide it well—I've had plenty of practice—but a girl from my youth group rats me out. The principal asks to smell my breath. *Sure*, I say, *Hhha. Hhha. Hhha.* Two months of Saturday detentions and a week of suspension. I don't mind: with the free time I ride my bike to McDonald's for breakfast, to the park for a nap. At night, I shave my head into a mohawk and pierce my own belly button with one of my mother's sewing needles.

In September, a postcard comes in the mail from the youth pastor at First Baptist Church, Brother Dan. He wants to know where I've been. He says everyone misses me. There's a concert coming up he thinks I might like to see. I toss it in the drawer of my desk. That night, I wait for my parents to go to bed. When all the lights blink out and I can hear them snoring, I tiptoe down the stairs in my underwear. I don't need clothes where I'm going. I don't lock the door behind me.

. . . . . .

After we put the hubcaps back on, we drive out to the lake. We're nearly out of booze and cigarettes. We park the car near the beach. One of the boys suggests we go skinny dipping. *The water's too cold*, Lauren says, looking a little sleepy. *I'll do it*, I say, pulling my shirt over my head, running barefoot toward the water. I can't feel a thing.

random facts

In the autumn of 1992, it started raining. It continued raining through the winter, until the rain turned to snow, and when spring came, the snow turned back to rain and kept falling. By summer, flooding began along the Mississippi and Missouri Rivers in Minnesota and South Dakota and Wisconsin before heading downstream to Iowa and Missouri, the rivers topping or breaking through levees along the way. Both the Mississippi and the Missouri swelled and left their banks, drowning first the low farmlands, then approaching the edges of towns, then filling the streets. The rain kept falling. Whole towns had to be relocated to higher ground. All told, the flood covered around thirty thousand square miles: fifteen million acres of farmland transformed into a disaster area. Some especially hard-hit areas along the Mississippi spent almost two hundred days under water.

. . . . .

Some version of a flood myth can be found in almost every culture. From the account of Tawa, the sun spirit in traditional Hopi mythology, who destroys the Third World with a great flood, to the Chinese story of Yu the Great, an emperor who tamed the rivers and lakes with the assistance of a dragon and a turtle, people on nearly every continent have reimagined their floods as acts of divine retribution. In the *Epic of Gilgamesh*, for example, one of the earliest known works of literature, Utnapishtim tells Gilgamesh that the gods have told him of their plan to flood the earth. The gods command him to build a boat, which he does, and loads it with everything he owns, including his relatives, slaves, and livestock. A terrible storm arrives, and, along with it, thunder and lightning and total darkness. All of the lesser gods climb to higher ground. On the seventh day, Utnapishtim opens a window in his boat and feels fresh air on his face.

· · · · ·

The story of Noah and the Ark is also well known.

· · · · ·

In every Baptist church at least one Sunday morning every year, ten or so children sit cross-legged on the floor, their Sunday school teacher sitting at the front of the room in a folding chair, holding a bright, laminated illustration on her lap: Good old Noah, a gentle-faced man with a long white beard, alone on the deck of his ship, a dove perched on his outstretched finger, an olive branch clutched in its foot: a symbol of God's promise never to destroy the earth again. And then, as the story goes, the waters receded, and old Noah and his family emerged from the ark onto a green mountainside. The sun was shining. God's gift: a beautiful day to start the whole world over again. A clean slate.

· · · · ·

James Robert Scott, a convicted arsonist and petty criminal, was convicted in 1994 of "intentionally causing a catastrophe" by removing several sandbags from a levee along the Mississippi River in Quincy, Illinois. As the river flooded fourteen thousand acres of farmland, destroying homes, businesses and area bridges, Scott boasted at a party about breaking the levee to strand his wife, Suzie, at her workplace across the river in Taylor, Missouri. His motivation, he said at the time, was a desire to fish, party, and have an affair. He is currently serving out a life sentence in the Jefferson City Correctional Center.

· · · · ·

The Bible I was given as a teenager tells it like this: *For forty days the flood kept coming on the earth, and as the waters increased they lifted the ark high above the earth. The waters rose and increased greatly, and the ark floated on the surface of the water. They rose greatly, and all the high mountains under the entire heavens were covered. The waters rose and covered the mountains. Every living thing that moved on the earth perished — birds, livestock, wild animals, all the creatures that swarm over the earth, and all mankind. Everything on dry land that had the breath of life in its nostrils died. Every living thing on the face of the earth was wiped out: men and animals and the creatures that move along the ground and the birds of the air. Only Noah was left, and those with him in the ark.*

. . . . .

Even as a child I knew that the land surrounding me was exceptionally beautiful: rolling pastures, green from April until December, wildflowers all summer long, untended trees growing up at the edge of every plot of land as a natural fence. It's a place that nurtured and sustained me as a child, a landscape that's restored me to happiness and tranquility time and time again as an adult. Say the word "Zion" to me and I'll think of that place. Then the water came, and the water was not beautiful but brown, undrinkable. Like what's left after washing dirty hands.

. . . . .

By the nineteenth century, biblical scholars had detected in the ark narrative two separate but complete and parallel stories. In both accounts, God grew angry with humankind, but in one version a pair of every kind of animal boards the ship; in the other version seven pairs of only the clean animals. In one version the flood is the result of rain; in the other version it comes from the primordial waters created in the separation of the earth from the firmament. The rains lasted forty days, and yet the waters rose for 150. The scholars collectively agreed that this was how the entire Pentateuch (Genesis, Exodus, Leviticus, Numbers, Deuteronomy—the first five books of the Bible) had been written: many authors spanning many centuries, separate sources combined into a single whole.

1993

The engines rev as we climb into the truckbeds, abandoning our cars at the water's edge. *We have to cross before the cops come.* A river you do not want to enter, water you should not drink: so quick to devastate, to murder even. The city girls beside us talk and talk, like puppets, like props. Who invited them? The driver shines his lights across the water; the truck lurches forward. The others will follow his lead. Everyone here has something to prove. The girl on the top of the wheel well leans toward us, her breath already so clear and sweet, asks, *How deep is the water?* asks, *What have you lost?* Her words hang in the air after she speaks them, no one daring to take them up, the night electrified by calculations. The driver speaks through the rear window while the water inches above the axle, the bumper, the top of the slow-moving wheel. *Don't worry,* he says, *She'll make it across.* Subtractions, subtractions: the creek bed washed away, a tractor underwater on its side, spilling its iridescent slick; a herd of bloated cattle floating under the bridge. At last the wheels catch dry gravel on the river's other side, the driver gunning it now, mud spraying behind the truck like a plume. The teenagers open the tailgates, pour into the ankle-high mud and trudge toward a dry island in the cornfield. In half an hour, a fire is burning—logs brought across the river, branches floated up on the new shore, planks from the roof of an old barn. The teenagers assemble their arsenal—three cases of Natural Light, twelve bottles of Boone's Farm, three bottles of Mad Dog 20/20, two bottles each of schnapps and Everclear. It's not sorrow we're trying to drown.

2006

ven before the flood, the neighbor tells me, *you heard rumors*. You sensed something dark was getting close, circling our town, picking people off one by one. The water was just an excuse. Families started moving out of houses. No one moved back in. A fight was always raging on the porch at that rundown rental across the street from the park. Then the rental was empty. The factory started cutting shifts—at first, only the graveyard. Then no more second shift. The younger adults moved to bigger towns to find work. Then the factory closed completely. Months later, the mines. Businesses downtown shut their doors on a Wednesday afternoon and didn't open on Thursday. First the jewelry store. Then the furniture store. Then the appliance store. Then the theater and the attorney's office and the pharmacy. By the end of the year, only the bar and the bank and the funeral house remained. *It's the same story all over these parts*. A town so small no one notices it's gone.

Growing up in this town, for me, was like learning to breathe underwater. Not that I was drowning from the start. On the farm, there was a whole universe in our backyard. Moving into the city limits, away from that, was like climbing into the bottom of a fishbowl and watching it fill up with water. Slowly. Slowly. Over years. Standing here, on our old front porch on Jackson Street, I'm haunted by my own ghost: walking from here straight west on Seward Street, past Judge Bell's sprawling neocolonial, past two blocks of massive Victorians, to Oakwood Cemetery, passing under that giant mausoleum, where headstones dated back centuries, their limestone facades nearly eroded away. At Oakwood Cemetery I could smoke and not get caught, could make out with a pimple-faced boy, or later, a grown man, could lean against an ancient oak tree sipping schnapps with my girlfriends, when I had them, or roll a joint, sit quietly by myself and pretend to be someplace else. I could hop on the freight train and get off in some place I'd never heard of, where no one would know me at all. And more than once I did exactly that: packed my bags and left my family and all of my friends. I changed my name, my address, became a different person. But something always pulls me, keeps pulling me, back to this exact spot over and over again.

ars poetica

s when a barn falls to the ground over decades, the boards rotting and sagging and giving way to gravity, the whole structure crumbling down and not a thing for it. As when a vine of lesser periwinkle creeps up the beams, along the rafters, out the roof, where it becomes a scramble of violet-purple, pale-purple, white-purple flowers (but only through the spring and summer months), choking out the rough-stalked weeds. Meanwhile the steeple of a church: its rust-silenced bell, its paint-flaking spire. As when the pastor stutters to a halt and a hydrangea blooms in the pit of your stomach (a shame, since no one sees it). As when it is raining. But it is not always raining. Meanwhile sparrows nest in a variegated weigela (which explains the small, winged seeds). Meanwhile every magnolia is blooming. And also that little dip at the base of my neck (what is the proper name for that place, that divot, that sinkhole, that sags and tautens and sags?). As when a train takes on its passengers. As in: their destinations. And yet some people also live in a place and belong there. Some people also live in a place and marry its simple boys with their sun-bleached hair and rough-calloused hands. Those men of few words. Meanwhile at least one magnolia doesn't bloom (we all have droughts). And at least one sparrow does not nest, but spends whole months darting in and out of cornfields near the highway, collecting twist-ties and cigarette butts and the quick-torn foil edges of elsewhere-discarded wrappers (a behavior I can't say I've ever seen) until the sudden and inexplicable strike of—not a clock, but an idea, a blessing of sorts: to fly, and fast, untouched through branches, brambles, leaves—a thicket, really. As when an idea forms and the child opens her mouth.

1994 . . . .

Fifteen minutes into the first day of the poetry unit, I'm bored senseless. Mrs. Harvey* has allowed us to choose among any number of Romantic poets — Blake, Wordsworth, Keats, Lord Byron, Browning — for silent reading period, and like most of my classmates, I've already grown bored and irritated; these poems are so far removed from my own language, my own experience, I feel small and stupid and poor. I close my book and walk toward the front of the room, where Mrs. Harvey copies notes from her lesson plan onto the blackboard in perfect cursive, not even turning to look at me when she says, *no, you may not use the restroom.* Back at my desk, I carve my name into the desk with a ballpoint pen, and rummage through my backpack before finally giving up: I close my eyes and open my book at random. I recognize the words:

> *The big doors of the country barn stand open and ready,*
> *The dried grass of the harvest-time loads the slow-drawn wagon,*
> *The clear light plays on the brown gray and green intertinged,*
> *The armfuls are pack'd to the sagging mow.*

. . . . .

Some time later I'm hunched over a notebook at the window in my room. I'm generally uninterrupted in the evenings, since my parents also occupy their private spaces. We no longer eat dinner together. My mom spends most of every day in her sewing room, her sewing machine occasionally whirring. If she is not sewing she is stuffing or ripping a seam. If she is not ripping a seam she is watching the news on her thirteen-inch television. Dad putters around the basement, moving boxes from the east side of the basement to the west, partially dismantling the washing machine, his socket set spread out on one side of the ping-pong table. I'm looking for a word I don't yet know. We don't have a thesaurus or a dictionary. My family doesn't own a computer. For hours I'll stare out the window, chaining synonyms toward a word I'll never reach.

The next day I give the poem to Mrs. Harvey, wring my hands while she reads it at her desk. I can't take my eyes off her face. She looks up, asks if I will read it to the class.

           • • • • •

> *I am there, I help, I came stretch'd atop of the load,*
> *I felt its soft jolts, one leg reclined on the other,*
> *I jump from the cross-beams and seize the clover and timothy,*
> *And roll head over heels and tangle my hair full of wisps.*

           • • • • •

Later that semester I write a paper on *The Great Gatsby*, enter it in an essay contest in AP English. It wins first prize.

whitegate drive . . . .

You try real hard to get good grades in college because you know exactly how much it cost but you work forty hours a week at Wal-Mart
and sometimes you're so damn tired you can't read the PSYCHOLOGY
open in front of you. Sometimes you don't know the words in front
of you but if you fake it your teachers always know that you are fak-
ing. Your mama calls and asks how you're doing and you tell her
you're doing great, Mama, just great and one day she calls to tell you
she has CANCER.* Your hands sweat and your knees tremble together
with every single one of your cousins and your aunts and uncles and
grandparents on both sides and both of your sisters in your mama's
hospital room holding hands around her bed while your daddy asks
the good Lord for STRENGTH. You don't even breathe until she's waking up from surgery with her mouth pawing open and each time you
look she is weaker and smaller and closer to dying and each time your
daddy palms his forehead he leaves tracks like the old creek bottom,
but now you know it's not just money he worries over, so you tell him
you'll drop out of school just till she's better but you don't plan to go
back for some time.

1996

It's nearing dark as I pull into the parking lot, where the streetlights flicker on and wheeze, casting a milk-green glow toward the building, where a line of rust-hooded cars buckle and lean downhill, toward the ditch, toward the east, toward the storm drain just this side of the street. From here I can see in all the windows, mostly unlit, the blinds left open all hours of the day, all the beige walls left bare — no nails or screws in the drywall, says the contract — each beige carpet stained by decades of itinerant boot tracks: from each bedroom to each kitchen to each bathroom and back. Smells from each floor drift into the stairwell: warm sudsy water from the laundry room, curry from a family I never see, stale beer and cigarette smoke from the college students on the third floor. My door is the third one down. My key is the one in the lock. Now it's closed behind me and the whole of my possessions makes a small pile in the corner of one room: a black trash bag stuffed full of clothes, a stack of books, a mirror, a lamp, three pairs of shoes, two of my grandmother's paintings. *I won't save anything for you*, my mother said while I packed in a rush. *I won't keep your room.* She didn't try to stop me. Dad didn't lend a hand, but before I could start the car, gave me a hammer and a bag full of nails. On the east wall I'll hang the bend in the road. On the west, the creek with stones.

white/trash

Except for each knuckle's wrinkle (petal pink, carnation bloom, sweet nothings in my ear) the body is divided, redivided into pale and paler versions (almond bark, whipping cream), not at all like the originary swatch (Easter glove, bridal veil, bleached beached shell). It stands in the shade of fulsome trees. Also: infinite cathedrals. An image which has no roots. Or has too many roots, which branch out and out forever, without a point of origin, without an original bulb from which the root system sprang, divided, and even in the beginning began to breed. An aberration, worse than inferior: a weed, which spreads, as across the surface of a body of water. Or as an infection spreads. An infestation. A plague. Except for the nutmeg marks (dysplastic nevi, dormant holocaust), you might ask me for directions. There is more than one right way. Johnson grass. Bermuda grass. Purple nutsedge. A mutation—not a mirror, but a split screen, where the first image is recognizable, and the other is at least partially repulsive. Not the Other, not exactly its opposite. Not even a third thing that lives between: a classification that defies classification, and each time makes it more invisible, inscrutable, inexplicable. Complete taxonomies gone missing, swallowed by an enormous, terrifying question, repeated, repeated, until the question is not a question, not of going blind, or of blending in. Not the color, not its skin, which is visible mostly to itself. But rather the slash that both precedes and follows, the division of the screens: a distance which allows the image to turn away from itself and say. Except for the broken slab of my back (*Gerbera jamesonii, Lilium longiflorum, Lavandula angustifolia*), you might introduce yourself. I have the bluest eyes you've ever seen.

2006

Before I've fully wrestled my grocery cart from the stack, the store has come to a halt: the checkout girls, the bag boys standing silent, staring in my direction. I've grown used to this: my pregnant belly ripening out in front of me, my arms and back covered in tattoos. I am a walking contradiction. Where I live, in Houston, such things are nearly commonplace. But here, it's a mark of my assimilation to the city and its values. It makes me uncomfortable, this staring. I rummage in my bag for my sweater, but I've left it in the car. In the produce section, I load the cart with bananas and pears, asparagus and sweet potatoes, grapes and ears of corn: all imported, brought in by the same roads I've traveled away from here and back. Even the corn, which I could buy in the parking lot out of the back of a truck from the farmer himself, is brought in on a semi from who-knows-where. At the meat counter a middle-aged woman *tsks* me loudly. Up and down the aisles stockers follow me with their stares. Inside my body, my daughter settles down to sleep. Protected. A woman who could be my grandmother calls me *trash* under her breath in the checkout line. At least we understand one another.

punchline*

At last he walks through the garage, enters the house through the laundry room and heads straight into the bathroom, where he unbuttons his shirt and tosses it into the laundry hamper, turns to wash his hands at the sink, brushes under his fingernails—the few he still has—though he knows they're a dirty that can't get clean with Lava soap, the better part of a century with his hands in the belly of greasy tractors. He dries with the pink towel she's hung by the mirror, takes the fresh shirt she's hung for him by the door: the same blue uniform every day. Without a word he sits at the kitchen table, waits for her to serve him. She's running only a few seconds behind, and just as he's about to look up from the table, she puts a plate in front of him. Frozen pizza again. *Supreme.* As always, cut into four small squares: two for her, two for him. They eat in silence with knives and forks, the corner of a peach cotton napkin tucked under each plate. In the front room, the police scanner issues only static. Some days, a fire or domestic disturbance. A drunk picked up and taken downtown in handcuffs, led across the clean green lawn for everyone to see. He looks at his plate while he's eating. She looks out the window.

1997

Seven aluminum crochet hooks, one for each dazzling hue of the visible spectrum, selected at length from the cluttered aisle of novice arts in the fluorescent-lit crafting store. It's nearly winter; Mom wears a brown suede coat, keeps putting packages in my arms: Wrights Aluminum Crochet Hook Set Sizes DEFGHIJ & K, three skeins of Red Heart Super Saver Jumbo Worsted Weight in 378 Claret, a copy of *Teach Yourself to Crochet in Just One Day*. She pays, smiles, and touches my arm (just once, gently) as she hands me the crisp plastic bag. We walk in silence to the cars. She asks if I need any money, tells me I look too thin. I don't tell her I am leaving. Or that the eighth hook is missing, misplaced somewhere among heaps of unusable colors, skeins too garish to be an integral part of any beautiful whole. Who would throw them away? Also: pounds of brittle glass beads, a knotted web of fishing twine, two spools of gold-colored wire, twelve untouched glue sticks, seventeen shades of all-purpose thread, twenty-two needles, and a pair of scissors equal parts steel and joy.

what I had on my sixty-third day
in New York City . . . .

Thirty-seven cents and two hands turned upward, a song in my throat the size of a fist, and a black leather boot print in the hungry storm of my stomach (empty but for a pair of crackers stolen from the soup kitchen, one piece of fruit, a napkinful of day-old bread); a summer dress that never hung but swelled around me in the slightest east-bound breeze, setting me adrift on a sea of catcalls, week-old newsprint, and a wave of dust sprung up from where? Not the thin streak of sky, gray and unbroken by even a single white-burning star; not the black cricket night but the steel-gray buzz of a long electric night; an avenue of taxi cabs coughing into the ridge of gangrene blisters on my street-stained feet (a photographer incised them in his studio bath; my tooth broke away on the spoon); the soot on my face streaked each day by a brief and glorious rain, more acid than water but I drank it anyway and understood even then that nothing is free

except a box of matches found in the muddy cradle of a tree, two half-smoked cigarettes plucked from a public sidewalk in the park; three nights spent under the miracle of a twin-sized cotton sheet, a velvet wingback chair all to myself—each morning an entire sunbeam in my lap, a waltz of bright-lit flecks, a lukewarm shower with no conditions whatsoever, and an unlocked door to the black asphalt roof undiscovered by anyone I knew, where the city loomed and kept on looming despite the static always firing between flesh and asphalt, plate glass windows and the reflection I kept expecting to see: instead a stranger, a street number, a bus briefly screeching to halt; *no, girl, don't you know nothing is free*

except seventeen loose sheets of blue-lined paper folded thickly in my pocket with the same ten words repeated over and over in a language I barely remember—*how can I go home? how can I ever return?*—the slant-starved scrawl heaving and toppling, each frantic letter crawling over the next toward a tangible and certain edge; a pay phone; a collect call; a bus ticket through the green promise of a continent, the space of my body, the air around it even, not just inside but beyond the shallow margin of my ten toes, two feet (and suddenly so strangely solitary), the habit of placing them one in front of the other, each time starting over again from the same patch of tree-buckled sidewalk, the same notched and crumbling curb, the front porch, the screen door, my finger once again on the bell, and yes, I carried even the past and future memory of that, and a single photograph of someone moving forward in opposite directions.

2006

If we were to visit the cemetery where my grandfather is buried* it would look exactly the way I remember it: crisp grass clipped short, the entrance set back from the road, sheltered from view by the shade of mature trees. But now the chapel would lean and sag, which I wouldn't remember, its windows broken and gaping. I would walk the rows of tombstones, not memorably longer than before, away from the entrance, trying to make out the names and dates, long since eroded. Even as a child I knew to stick to the paths, keep my feet off the graves. It's a rule that doesn't need explaining. At last I would find the plot: my grandfather's final resting place. My grandmother will also be buried here when she dies. They bought the twin plots ages ago. Her current husband, the man I've always known as Grandpa, will be buried next to his first wife, miles away from here on a quiet hill, where cows graze in the surrounding pastures. I don't envy that difficult decision: to choose one loved husband over another, the past over the present. I would touch the headstone—the marble so cold even in the blistering heat—and we would head back to the car.

When the winding blacktop intersects the highway, I tell my husband I want to be cremated. *Scatter my ashes at the river's edge*, I say. Let them twist and tumble me between these hills, settle me along the river bottom, drift me out to sea. I always come to this same conclusion: To live I have to leave.

still life with picture window

At last he turns into the gravel driveway, the white rocks popping as the tires drop from the blacktop, pulls around the house's west side, stopping at the concrete slab bridging the distance between the gravel and the back door. He kills the engine and pats her leg before coming around to her side, opening her door, taking her hand, her elbow, pulling her up and out of the car. She's more sure of her footing on the concrete, crosses to the house — the back door always unlocked — her tiny dog rushes in circles around her feet, while her husband gathers the parcels from the trunk. He carries them past her into the house and up the back stairs, lifts them to the kitchen counter, places the bacon in the fridge, brings the books into the living room and stacks them neatly by her chair. She waits at the door while the dog sniffs and scratches at a dandelion in the lawn — *Hurry up and do your business!* The dog darts in a wide circle around the house before following her up the stairs to the giant recliner in the living room. She sits, the dog perching beside her on the chair's wide arm. At last her husband sits on the couch beside her and turns on the television, keeps the volume down low so as not to disturb her reading. She pulls the lever on the left side of her chair, the footrest flies up, and she leans over to pick up the first book on the pile, her glasses sliding down to the end of her nose as she inspects the book's spine, its front and back covers, the title page. At last he dozes, begins snoring. She clears her throat; the words come into focus.

2001

Under the spotlight I can't see the audience, though there is the smell of wine. The dirty dishes clacking together in a faraway kitchen sink. The cigarette smoke, thick like in the movies, as when someone taps the microphone, says, is this thing on? It's on: there is also the sound of my breathing, amplified, the slip of paper rattling out of my pocket, my hands rattling to open it. *Hi there*, I say into the restless dark, its legs uncrossing and recrossing. The waitress delivers an order: Grey Goose martini, very dirty, extra olives; old vine zin. Please don't laugh me off the stage. Please don't make me take off my clothes, unfasten my bra, turn my back and dance on someone's lap. I'm so naked already. Let me open my mouth. *Deity,** I say, my voice small and acorn-hard. *I can feel you.* Boiled-egg hard *in the back of my throat.* Jello-mold hard *in the place that I begin the word "god."* Cotton-ball hard, but hollowing as a figure in the front row stands, turns, walks toward the door. *I hate that.* There is also the scuffed toe of my boot, and the fingernails, which are chewed and peeling. Look at the sweat stains, the mismatched buttons, the mismatched thread. The hair I cut myself. *You create me.* There is also the floor, I think, where shoes dangle from the darkness, tied and polished and shining. *Each time you speak my name.* The silhouettes shift, put down their glasses. And then there is silence like thunder. No one is laughing. They're clapping. Amen.

2004

I'm crossing the Broadway Bridge back into downtown Kansas City. It's a gorgeous spring day, even more gorgeous because I'm high on adrenaline after three hours under my tattooist's needle. I've got the windows of my Monte Carlo rolled down, a lit cigarette between my fingers; a song I know plays on the radio. I sing along loudly. My phone rings; I don't recognize the number, answer without rolling up the windows, shouting loudly into the receiver: HELLOOOOO! *Yes, this is Adam Zagajewski calling for Lacy Johnson.* I roll the windows up without throwing out my cigarette, my voice box having descended to my stomach, my car filling with smoke. Gulp. This is she. *Yes, I am calling to inform you that you have been accepted to the Creative Writing Program at the University of Houston . . .* I am shocked, stunned. Flabbergasted. This is the fourth time I've applied to the program, and this time I applied feeling certain I'd get the rejection letter in early April. Ohmygod thankyousomuch I say and quickly hang up the phone, just as I hear him begin to speak again. I've just hung up on Adam Zagajewski, but I won't realize it until hours later.

I find a spot in the parking garage, rush into the building, up the stairs to the apartment I now share with my new boyfriend—my mother calls it *living in sin.* It was his place when we met—a one-bedroom loft on the second floor of the building between a divey sportsbar and the corner store where we buy cigarettes every morning and soda and beer every evening, when we've got the money. I put my key in the lock—it sticks every time—and I bang and turn and jingle and knock until he comes to let me in. I blurt out the news—HOUSTON!—without saying hello. He's already agreed to move with me wherever I am accepted to graduate school, if I am accepted to graduate school. He gives me a high-five, a hug, heads to the kitchen to grab me a beer as I shout out the window: *I'm going to be fucking famous!*

When I call my dad he congratulates me. *That's great news, honey.* When I call my mom she wants to know if she was the first person I called. *Well . . . no.* She cries and hangs up the phone. That night, I lie awake fantasizing about the day I will appear on Oprah. She will put her hand on my knee: *This is all so beautiful.*

The day before the move, my sisters come over to help us pack. Though they don't so much help as keep me company. Leeanne sits on the couch and pets one of our cats. Lisa makes cracks about all the boxes of books. I order pizza. Josh runs down to the corner store for beers.

In the morning, Dad arrives to say goodbye. He helps load the last few things into the trailer. He doesn't say so, but he isn't so keen on me moving to Texas, especially with a man I'm not married to, especially since I met him only a few months ago. Mom says so: *I want you close to home.* She doesn't come to say goodbye, especially since she knows my dad is coming, and they've been doing their best to avoid one another ever since the divorce. Naively, I've continued to try to find ways to get them in the same place: Christmas at my sister's house, a birthday party, my graduation from the master's program at the University of Kansas. But this isn't *Parent Trap* and they're not reconciling. They've both remarried. They're both much happier now.

More than once my father breaks down in tears: when I answer the door of our empty apartment, a pink handkerchief over my hair, a pair of flight goggles pushed up on my forehead; at lunch, which he buys, when we raise our glasses and toast to the future, the long road that lies ahead; when I hug him, kiss his cheek, promise I'll be back soon, because that won't be soon enough; when I close the door, fasten my seatbelt, and roll down my window; when we pull the car down the alley, around the corner, onto the street, the on-ramp, the interstate, and all the while I'm waving out the window.

2005

Early in my second year of the creative writing PhD program at the University of Houston, I am invited to give a reading at Brazo's Bookstore as a part of the *Gulf Coast* Reading Series. To promote the event, I am interviewed on KUHF's *The Front Row*. The next day the interview is made available online, and I send a link to several of my family members, including my father, who is one of the few people to actually listen to it. I call him, hoping to get his reaction, thinking he'll be brimming with pride. *You've got it all wrong*, he says a little shortly. *You don't understand us at all.*

That night, a Saturday, one of my girlfriends throws me a party to celebrate my twenty-seventh birthday. It is attended by every person in Houston I know. At midnight a crowd sings me Happy Birthday, and I blow out candles on the beautiful, store-bought cake. They urge me to give a toast. I say something grateful, sophisticated. My boyfriend interrupts, his hand in his pocket, tells me he has something he'd like to add. He clears his throat, a velvet box in his outstretched hand.

We are married in Houston in January. My parents attend the ceremony, along with their new spouses, but neither of my sisters and none of my extended family are able to make it. In March we fly to Belize for a belated honeymoon. On the porch of our cabana we make plans to travel the world. *I want to spend a year in Ireland*, I say. *I'll get a Fulbright to study Joyce and learn to speak and read Irish.* My husband wants to spend a year in Africa or Japan. I'll be rich and famous by then, we joke. We can live without family for years on end, we say. We won't need a reentry plan.

When we return to Houston, I am pregnant with our first child. And all I can think of is going home.

2006

We've already said our goodbyes: spent one last evening at dinner with my mom and her husband, one last lunch with my dad and his wife. My father hugged me a long time in the parking lot, told me he loved me, and to drive safe. My mom put her hands on my belly, leaned her face close, and shouted, *I love you in there!* We spend our last night in the empty living room, our camcorder hooked up to the thirteen-inch television, watching the interviews from the relative comfort of the two folding chairs, laughing a little at the sound of our recorded voices, how frequently we break down in tears. After my husband goes to bed I move through the house, looking in empty closets, sit in the middle of my old bedroom, now comfortably air-conditioned, with plush, clean carpeting. From the back porch I can see the stars, even through the pollution of the streetlights. Not as bright as from the farm—where the whole galaxy, and our small place within it, shone evident on every clear night—but bright enough to make out the major constellations. Tomorrow we'll wake up early, before the sun rises even, and pack the last of the suitcases into the Jeep, leave the key inside the house, and lock the door behind us. By sunset we'll be back in our apartment in Houston, which is not home exactly, but neither is this house which is not my house. This town which is not my town. Not anymore. The child growing inside me begins hiccupping. Her life stretches out before me like the road away from here.

university heights

Your mama puts your picture in the paper when you go back to school. You take classes with black folks and brown folks and yellow folks and make friends with who you like. Your parents take you out to dinner with your sisters and when your daddy is halfway through with his second beer and his cheeks are glowing with the red blood rushing to his face he lifts his glass and says that he is proud of you. When he finishes his third beer he goes out to sleep in the car and your mama gives you three brand-new black pens and a pad of Post-its from her purse. You study real damn hard this time because you know this is your last earthly chance to make something of yourself and you buy a dictionary at a yard sale and think you might learn every word if you have DETERMINATION and RESOLVE. When Wal-Mart doesn't let you off to study for a test you tell them to kiss your poor white ass and you apply for student loans and when they give out credit cards on campus you accept exactly three. Your English professor says you have POTENTIAL and you hold this real close to your heart when you're walking up to get your diploma and every one of your cousins and your aunts and uncles and grandparents on both sides and your two sisters are hooting and hollering from the stands and your mama blows an air horn and your daddy yells your name so loud and true it's like he's calling you to come up from the creek bottom. And you hear him calling for some time.

Notes

Page xi: Here's something true: my first year of graduate school I read an essay by Mary Louise Pratt—"Arts of the Contact Zone"—in which Pratt defines "autoethnography" as "a text in which people undertake to describe themselves in ways that engage with representations others have made of them." Her example of this kind of text is a twelve-hundred-page letter written in 1613 by Felipe Guaman Poma de Ayala, an indigenous Andean, to King Philip III of Spain, using a combination of Spanish and Quechua, employing both written text and captioned line drawings. By engaging with what he perceived to be chronic misrepresentations of his culture in the letters that Spanish conquistadores were writing to an audience of the literate elite back home in Spain, Guaman Poma created a new, more complicated representation: a mirror of the Spanish culture as he saw it, an idealized reflection of his own.

Page 1: *Farm*, from the Old English *feorm*, is a word not found outside the English language. An early meaning of the word may have been *fixed portion* (of provisions or rations). Later derivations, such as *feormian*, signified *to feed*. Etymologists have proposed an alternate origin in the Latin *firma*, a word which can be found in the most ancient poetry, confirming its very ancient use.

Page 2: It's not the only time I have this argument. There was also the summer I lived in New York City. At a party in someone's cramped one-bedroom apartment, a woman from New Jersey with mall bangs made a remark about my southern accent. *Missouri isn't southern*, I said. The woman laughed in my face. And there was also the time, much later, when my boss's husband mentioned he had moved to the area from "back East" (for what purpose I don't know) and hated it. I told him he just didn't understand. He cleared his throat, turned to the person next to him, and changed the subject.

Page 3: Quail meat, even from wild quail, has a delicate nutty flavor, and is generally red and sweet, as compared to other wild game. Two quail make an appropriate main course for one adult person.

Frog legs, by contrast, are often said to taste like chicken because of their mild, chicken-like flavor and firm, chicken-like texture. Frog legs are considered a delicacy in many parts of the world, including eastern Europe, China, and Indonesia. In the United States, frog legs are most popular in Cajun cuisine and in the South, where bullfrogs and leopard frogs are most abundant.

Page 4: Jimtown is not exactly a town. At one time or another, there was a school, a general store, and a cemetery, which was all that was needed for a crossroads to count as a town in those parts. The school, which my father and his brother and sister all attended, is located just down the road from my grandmother's house, and is the only Jimtown building still standing. After all the one-room schools in the area were consolidated in the early sixties, the Jimtown school was converted into a private residence.

Page 4: Wilda (Johnson) Hoover, née Welsh, my father's mother, admitted to me that because of the dubious nature of their elopement, her marriage to my grandfather was probably not legal. *It was legal in God's eyes, though. And that's all that mattered.* Before the simple civil ceremony the judge asked, *Eighteen?* She replied, *Mmph.* Which was not exactly a lie.

Page 6: In 1935, FDR created the Rural Electrification Administration with the primary goal of bringing electricity to farms. At that time, nearly 90 percent of rural homes were unpowered, primarily due to the unwillingness of private electric utilities to extend their lines outside of urban areas. The rural market was largely ignored because high construction costs outweighed the limited profits such an investment would return. This is not to say, however, that power companies were completely unwilling to power rural areas: customers could connect to the electric grid if they advanced the financing for the necessary infrastructure, and if they were willing to pay electrical rates twice as high as urban rates. Because few farmers in the Great Depression could afford to meet these conditions, rural residents continued on as they had always done: without power. Rural life thus became increasingly different from urban and suburban life — without electricity, farmers had no use for other modern conveniences: telephones, radios, refrigerators, washing machines, hot water heaters, and other household appliances.

Although the REA was not directly involved in stringing the power lines — it was, rather, primarily a financial institution — the agency was largely responsible for the creation of rural electric cooperatives: not-for-profit consumer-owned firms organized to provide electric service to member-customers. A central board established rates and policies for the entire cooperative. By 1942, almost 50 percent of farms had electricity; nearly all by the early 1950s. Electrical service for farms brought with it access to mass communication: radio was followed by television, and over time these media began to narrow the cultural, educational, and commercial divide between urban and rural America.

Page 6:

PORTRAITS
By James J. Metcalfe

MY LOVE IS YOURS
I think of you all day and I
Adore you in my dreams
With every bit of love in me
However poor it seems
I want to do so much for you
I know not where to start
Except as I have said before
To offer you my heart
I want to send you gifts of gold
And call at your address
With parcels wrapped in faith and hope
and filled with happiness
I want to praise and honor you
And under every star
I want to tell the whole wide world
How wonderful you are
Oh, let me take you in my arms
And hold you close to me
And let me touch my lips to yours
And kiss you tenderly.

Page 11: Laura Anna Webber, née Everman, did not tell me this story. During the interview with my mother's parents, I could barely get either one of them to say much of anything at all. When my grandfather took my husband out to his shop, I finally got my grandmother to admit that her main chore had been milking the cows. And that she met my grandfather because he was her father's milk tester. At that time she slept in a room with five of her sisters, three to a full-sized bed. All of the other information I gleaned from stories my mother told me and from my grandmother's photographs. In one family portrait, taken probably in the early sixties, she's kneeling in the lawn with her hands in her lap, just in front of her mother, who's seated in a chair beside her husband, the other siblings variously seated or kneeling or standing in typical family portrait formation. Behind them: a corner of their modest home, its white siding clean and well-maintained, the windows open, the drapes drawn back. My grandmother is the only person in the photograph who looks modern — a smart blue dress with a nipped-in waist and a silver costume brooch. She's also the only person in the photo not looking into the camera. Instead she looks at someone or something out of the frame. Her expression can only be described as incredulous.

Page 12: I didn't know it at the time, but my great-grandparents (my father's paternal grandparents), owned not only this house in Livonia, but also the general store. During the Great Depression, my father told me, a grocery store was a profitable business, and the Johnsons were one of the wealthiest families around. They were the first family in town to own an automobile, and were not shy about driving it wherever they needed to go. To understand the extravagance of this fact, I should point out that a person can nearly spit from one end of Livonia to the other. As of the 2000 census, the village had a population of 114 and occupied an area of six blocks by five blocks, or less than one square mile.

Page 15: My grandmother named my mother Judith Marlene Webber, after Marlene Dietrich, whose beauty she greatly admired. In fact, my grandmother named both of her children after famous actors: her son, my uncle, is Kirk Douglas Webber.

Page 17: Although my aunt and uncle, who lived in Marceline, Missouri, owned a satellite TV, most homes in the area used aerial antennas to tune in to television broadcasts. Changing the channel was, for us, an undertaking, since it took nearly thirty seconds to rotate the antenna forty-five degrees. Often, we would change the channel on the television and peer through the static to see if the program was worth the effort of rotating the antenna to bring the station into focus. When we moved to the house on Jackson Street, my parents ordered basic cable, which seemed to my sisters and me like an incredible luxury. We moved into the house in time to catch reruns of *The Real World: New York* on MTV, and to see the last episode of *Cheers*, and, the following year, the premier of *Friends*, but to this day I have never seen an episode of *The Brady Bunch*, which appeared in the 1980s only in syndication.

Page 21: This description is based on Special D Meats, a "Full Service Butcher Shop" located just north of Macon, Missouri, at the corner of US Highway 63 and what is now Lake Street, though during my childhood this gravel road was known only as Rural Route One. The services provided by Special D Meats include custom slaughtering and processing (of beef, hogs, lambs, elk, and buffalo), a complete catering service (including menu items such as "whole hog roast"), a deer-processing service (in operation through gun season in November), and a retail area, where customers can purchase homemade smoked meats, sausages, and cheeses, fresh pork and beef, cut daily, as well as frozen beef and pork cuts, lamb, buffalo, elk, fruit, fish, and "variety meats."

Page 22: This is a clear exaggeration, though I did, in fact, find myself at the altar on many occasions. An essential part of any Southern Baptist church service is the invitational, when the congregation is invited to come up to the front of the church, repent of their sins, and commit their lives to Jesus. It wasn't so much the preacher's words that got under my skin, but rather the hymn, which more often than not was "Just as I Am." Invariably, by the time the congregation got to the refrain, "O Lamb of God, I come. I come," I found myself sobbing and walking down the aisle.

Page 25: Although my father's paternal grandfather suffered from Charcot-Marie-Tooth, a degenerative disease of the nerves in the feet and legs, his bandages were the result of more than one hundred surgeries he had undergone as treatment for osteomyelitis, a chronic infection of the bone and bone marrow. My uncle recalled that because his father, Arthur Jr., had spent most of his adolescence and adulthood caring for his ailing father, Arthur Sr.—*who could do very little in the way of throwing a ball or fishing or hunting with his son*—Arthur Jr. spent more time with his children than was typical of fathers at that time. Wilda recalled that her husband would get up with the babies in the middle of the night and rock them, singing "Hey! Ba-Ba-Re-Bop," slapping their backs to the beat. *I thought a little too roughly*, she told me, *but they always went back to sleep*. Arthur Sr. died in 1953. This is the only memory my father has of him.

Page 29: Neither of my parents had indoor plumbing in their houses until the late 1950s, which meant that each not only bathed in a galvanized tub in the kitchen of their home, but also that each had to venture to the outhouse, far away from the actual house. My mother confessed that she spent many winters very constipated out of reluctance to go outside in the bitter cold. She claimed that many people died from a similar affliction, though I can find no published evidence of this. My father also recalled burning his elbow very badly on the potbelly stove during a bath one evening. My grandmother denies this, since the potbelly stove was in the living room, and she only ever bathed her children in the kitchen.

Page 32: I realized, only as I was working on this book, that my grandmother, my mother's mother, is the better businessman of the family. Whereas nearly every business my grandfather ever ran—his farm, a tractor-repair shop, a fireworks stand—failed (except for his current business, which he runs out of his garage), my grandmother has succeeded at nearly everything she's tried. *Did you ever think of that?* she asked, turning to him during the interview. He gave her a long hard look then looked away. *Mmph.*

From bits and pieces of other, indirect stories, I gather that she began working out of the house only after my grandfather lost the farm. At first she worked only odd jobs: as a waitress, sorting chicks at the chicken farm, managing the accounting in the office at the chicken farm. Then she bought a restaurant, which was profitable for many years. My mother waited tables there during her lunch break from school, and in the afternoons and evenings. During this time my grandfather was driving to Milan, a nearby town, to work for the John Deere tractor company, and in the mid- to late sixties they bought the house they live in now. Then one day the restaurant burned to the ground. Or they sold it. My grandparents later built several storage units in Unionville, which has been a lucrative business for decades. My grandmother handles the books.

Page 36: Despite being "just a corner on the side of the road," Lemons, Missouri, is an actual town located south of Unionville, Missouri, at the junction of Highway 5 and State Highway B. It consists of a cemetery, several houses, and a three-story building locals refer to as the county farm, a former asylum rumored to be haunted. Ghost chasers have reportedly recorded some "pretty strange footage" there. Visitors are cautioned to be careful of the owner, who lives directly across the road and who does not take kindly to trespassers, and also to be careful of the collapsing floors.

Page 39: This line comes from the Langston Hughes poem "You and Your Whole Race." I am certain we did not, in fact, read this poem in class. I am also certain that Langston Hughes was one of the very few black authors I encountered during formal public schooling. What is more likely is that we read the poem "Harlem," also known as "A Dream Deferred," a poem that is more agreeable to public school officials because it does not point fingers. Hughes was born in Joplin, Missouri, which is near the southwest corner of the state, roughly 260 miles as the crow flies from my home in Macon, Missouri, in the central northern part of the state.

Page 39: I should note that my parents now, and to a certain degree even then, recognize that they were wrong in the way they treated my sister. They did eventually reconcile, though only after she broke up with her boyfriend and moved back into our house. She was home only maybe a few weeks before landing a job at a McDonald's near the mall in Columbia, Missouri, a college town about sixty miles south of Macon. When I moved out of the house at seventeen, I moved in with her. By that time she was working at a record store in the mall, and I found a job at the Wal-Mart SuperCenter across town. I could have worked at the Wal-Mart by the mall near our apartment, in an otherwise empty strip mall that would be demolished a decade later, but I didn't want people to think I was trashy.

Page 44: We bought this horse, a Tennessee Walker named Ebony, several months before we also bought her brother, Dusty, a much larger gelding I was too scared to ride. From day one, the horses hated to be apart. If we tried to ride them separately, the one left behind would gallop to the end of the pasture, stopping just short of the fence, stamping and whinnying until its sibling came back into sight. Only after we moved into town and sold both horses did we learn that for years Ebony had been suffering from moon blindness, or uveitis, a recurrent, painful inflammation or infection of one or both eyes, which often eventually results in total blindness.

Page 45: Among the smells my mother tells me she cannot tolerate, dead chicken feathers is one of the worst, but pig shit tops the list. She's not the only one: in 2002 seven families living near Berlin, Missouri, filed suit against the industrial hog producer Premium Standard Farms. The plaintiffs complained that relentless and extreme odors emanating from the defendant's 4,300-acre finishing farm—where nearly two hundred thousand hogs are fattened and slaughtered each year—prevented them from leaving the house. The judge found in favor of the plaintiffs, ordering Premium Standard Farms to pay eleven million dollars in damages.

By contrast, the best smell, my mother tells me, is that of horses, or of a baby lamb that is born too early and has fallen asleep in a box behind the wood-burning stove. *That smell—the smell of warm little lambs—is one of those things you never can forget.*

Page 56: A few words from my mother about my great-grandmother, her paternal grandmother: *I can remember when [my brother] Kirk was born I had to go stay with them, and she tried to give me a bath in the galvanized tub and we had to go to the bathroom in a pot in the house and then she tried to make me wear these long black socks that went clear up to my thighs. I don't know why. Because that was the way she dressed, I guess. One of the other things I can remember her doing was she'd put Vaseline all over her face and then put a plastic bag over the Vaseline—wrap her face in a plastic bag—and she'd sleep that way. But she wasn't the type that cared about her appearance. So why she went to all this trouble to not have the wrinkles, I don't know. But I also remember she made the best fried cornbread, and they had that every meal. My grandpa would have a glass of milk and he'd put that cornbread in his milk. Every Sunday all the sons and daughters would come home and their kids would go out and play and the grownups would sit around and talk. But they were also real religious and so my grandma tried to push that on me, too. My mom and dad, we went to church for a while, until she just got so fanatic that it turned my mom and dad against it altogether.*

Page 58: Although my father undoubtedly listened almost exclusively to conservative talk radio, the only program I remember is Paul Harvey's *The Rest of the Story*, a weekday newscast consisting of purportedly factual reportage on a variety of subjects with a surprise element (the corner druggist's liver tonic is really Coca-Cola!) saved until the end. I loved these formerly untold histories: a more interesting version of the past lingering just under the surface of everyday life. After Paul Harvey gave away the surprise, he concluded each episode with the tag line "And now you know . . . the *rest* of the story."

Page 65: My father confessed: *Most people don't have the good fortune of knowing that young what they want to do, but I knew then that I wanted to be an aeronautical engineer. I was forced into it by the hot dirty job of hauling hay. And I did not want to do that for the rest of my life.* He did not, in fact, go on to be an aeronautical engineer, since the University of Missouri–Columbia did not at that time have a program in aeronautical engineering. He settled on being a mechanical engineer instead.

Page 67: Whether it was due to my poor shot, or lack of interest, I can't recall, but this was the only time I ever went hunting with my father. We came back empty-handed that day, but on other occasions I remember my father returning with enough small birds to feed our family for dinner, handing them over to my mother to pluck the feathers and dress the carcasses.

Page 71: My mother admits that she was unkind to her younger brother, who struck her as boring and bookish. When he graduated from high school, several years behind her, he joined the army, and spent much of his adult life overseas. There are two photographs of him in uniform, about to ship out to some distant shore: in one, he's standing beside my grandmother in the front room of their house—he looks somber, she looks devastated; in the other, he's standing beside my grandfather, a veteran himself; the son's hands are at his sides, the father's in his pockets.

Page 80: Although KAAY currently plays contemporary Christian music, in the sixties it played Top 40 hits until late evening, when Clyde Clifford played several hours of underground music on his program, *Beaker Street*. Frequency 1090 was also shared by XERB, where Wolfman Jack played early rock-and-roll records from Rosarito Beach, Mexico, though the station claimed to be based in Hollywood, California. In the mideighties, religious broadcasters purchased the station, and KAAY dropped its slogan, "The Mighty 1090."

Page 82: This story ran in the *Unionville Republican* next to an advertisement for Dorothy's Beauty Salon, the announcement of a Special Cattle Sale, and a Financial Statement of the Shoal Creek Drainage System. In the photograph, "by Putnam," both my parents smile toothily. They look radiant and happy. And also impossibly young: they hadn't yet turned nineteen.

Page 97: My grandfather, Arthur William Johnson Jr., died on October 7, 1978, at Ellis Fischel Cancer Center. Everyone knew he was near the end, and my father had already been to the hospital to say his goodbyes. On the day of his death, my father got the call that the time had come, and packed us all into the conversion van. He drove nearly eighty miles an hour, trying to reach the hospital in time. As he neared Kirksville, Missouri, nearly ninety miles north of Columbia, he stopped racing, slowing the van down to the speed limit. *I knew in my heart—in the deepest part of my soul—that I was too late.*

Page 101: The Parable of the Lost Son appears in Luke 15:11–32 and is the last of the three parables on redemption Jesus relates to his followers. The story goes like this: the younger of two sons asks his father for his inheritance, which readers are to understand as an insult: the equivalent of wishing his father were dead. The son travels far and wide, wasting his money in extravagant living. Eventually he has to take work as a pig herder, and when he reaches the point of envying the pigs, he comes to his senses and returns home. His father welcomes him with love and generosity, far more than he has a right to expect, treating him as an honored guest. The older son, who has stayed at home to work in his father's fields, resents the reception his brother receives and questions his father. The parable concludes with the father explaining that a celebration is necessary because the younger son "was dead, and is alive again. He was lost, and now is found!"

Page 101: Everclear is the brand name of a clear, colorless, tasteless, highly concentrated pure grain alcohol. It is combined with vodka, peach schnapps, rum, apple schnapps, Triple Sec, gin, Apple Pucker, Boone's Farm Strawberry Hill, orange juice, Hawaiian Punch, Sprite, and fresh fruit to make a party drink called Jungle Juice. It can be combined with Countrytime Lemonade mix and Mountain Dew to make a drink called Antifreeze. Its sale is illegal in many states. Missouri is not one of them.

Page 110: I learned only in the process of writing this book that my former teacher Denise Harvey died earlier this decade. I can find no information about her death, but only that a memorial scholarship has been created in her honor. Application instructions include the following: *At some time in our lives we have all been made to feel bad by someone's hurtful remarks. We have also at some time in our lives been made to feel special because someone took the time to lift our spirits by their words or actions. Tell us about an incident when you were lifted up by someone's kindness.*

Page 112: Both my mother and a woman she knew from church were diagnosed with breast cancer around the same time. *I didn't know-know her, she says, but she always struck me as a good person. A good Christian woman.*

But the other woman didn't survive. *And I didn't think that was fair.* The lucky woman felt a stabbing pain in her breast, had a mammogram, a biopsy, a mastectomy, double reconstruction. *It was the aggressive kind. If I had let it go it would have been another story. Wouldn't have taken any time.* The whole process—from stabbing pain to mastectomy—took only a couple of weeks. The reconstruction took much longer, was much more painful—pulling the muscles away from where they were used to growing, stuffing them full of saline-filled pouches, going in each week to have more fluid injected into them. *And your dad was not really there for me.* She woke up from surgery and went into convulsions when she felt the pain, again when the doctor started taking out the stitches, when she saw her missing breast. *I felt like I was all alone. I was so ashamed but what choice did I have? It was that or die.*

Page 116: An alternate title for this chapter might be *joke in which the punchline is not funny.*

Page 120: My grandfather is buried in St. John's Cemetery in Livonia, Missouri. Out of a total of 746 interments, the earliest legible burial date is 1849, ten years before the original town plat was surveyed in 1859. In *History of Adair, Sullivan, Putnam, and Schuyler Counties, Missouri, from the Earliest Times to the Present,* a thick illustrated volume printed by the Goodspeed Publishing Company in 1888, the anonymous authors include the following information about Livonia: [In 1859] *it consisted of four blocks of eight lots each. One street ran through the center of the town from north to south, and one likewise through the center from east to west. This is where the town was first laid off. There were a few families living on the town site; but when [the original town proprietor] died the post-office was moved to a farm . . . about three miles north of its original location. It is now located on Section 19, Township 66, Range 16. Joseph Martin is the postmaster and merchant. Dan Kelley is the blacksmith, and the population consists of three families, or about fifteen persons.* That earliest tombstone, the one from 1849, bears the following inscription: *Dau. of S. and J.—1y, 6m.* The inscription on my grandfather's tombstone gives his name, the date he was born, the date he was married, the date he died.

Page 122: Thanks to the former editors of the now defunct literary magazine *Ardentia,* where this poem first appeared, in a slightly altered form. Thanks also to the editors of *Memoir (and)* and *Sentence,* where earlier versions of portions of this manuscript have appeared in print and/or as audio performances. Thanks to Mark Doty, Claudia Rankine, John Weir, and Rubén Martinez for being thoughtful and compassionate teachers, and to Joshua Rivkin, Casey Fleming, and Kelly Secovnie for being good readers and good friends. Thanks to Christine Jensen Sundstrom, Ron Wilson, Brian Lagotte, and Leslie Head for hearing me out. Thanks to Joseph Parsons and the entire editorial staff of the University of Iowa Press for believing in this book before I had even written it. Thanks to Judy Mathis, Barry Johnson, Brenda and Terry McMillan, Bruce and Brenda Johnson, Wilda and Ralph Hoover, and Harold and Laura Webber for opening your homes and your hearts to me and this project. Thanks for the generous financial support of the Kansas Arts Commission, a state agency, and the National Endowment for the Arts, a federal agency. And thanks to my husband, Josh Okun, for the generous gift of his time, talents, and loving partnership.

sightline books . . . .
The Iowa Series in Literary Nonfiction